MW00580767

The
According to Mark

A Latin-English,
Verse-by-Verse Translation

Translated by John Cunyus

ISBN #: 978-0-9824802-9-8

©2010, John G. Cunyus
All Rights Reserved to Images, Commentary, and Translation reserved.
www.JohnCunyus.com.

Latin text from *Biblia Sacra Iuxta Vulgatam Versionem*,
Fourth Revised Edition, edited by Roger Gryson,
© 1994 Deutsche Bibelgesellschaft, Stuttgart.
Used by permission.

Searchlight Press
Who are you looking for?
Publishers of thoughtful Christian books since 1994.
PO Box 482
Glen Rose, Texas 76042
888.896.6081
info@Searchlight-Press.com
www.Searchlight-Press.com
www.JohnCunyus.com

Manufactured in the United States of America

To Myles Hall

Introduction to Mark

Who: Since at least the early 2nd Century of the Common Era, this gospel has been associated with John Mark, a younger companion both of Peter and Paul, though Mark's name does not appear in the text of the gospel itself. Mark, in all probability a trilingual Jew, was living in Jerusalem at the home of his mother Mary when first mentioned in Acts 12:12. His first language would have been Aramaic, also the native tongue of Jesus. As part of his education, Mark would have learned some Hebrew. In his interaction with non-Jews, he relied on the *Koine Greek* that was the common idiom in the eastern half of Rome's empire.

Mark joined Paul and Barnabas on their first missionary journey, though he apparently did not complete the trip. After a controversy between Paul and Barnabas over Mark for having abandoned the journey, Barnabas and Paul parted ways and Mark continued with Barnabas. As 2 Timothy 4:11 points out, Mark's relationship with Paul was repaired at the end. Traditionally, the gospel was thought to be a record of Peter's reminiscences and proclamation. Peter mentions Mark as his "son," in 1 Peter 5:13.

Given his frequent asides explaining Jewish customs, Mark seems to address an audience that is unfamiliar with them and thus, by inference, is not primarily Jewish. The presence of Latin loan words in Greek, such as "centurion," reinforces the sense that non-Jews were being addressed.

What: The literary genre Mark pioneers is called gospel. The document was originally written in *Koine* or "Common" *Greek*, the trade language of the eastern Roman empire in the 1st Century CE. Mark's written language is unpolished, almost crude. The document represents two crucial points in the development of Christianity: 1. It represents the transition from a free-flowing, oral, story-telling tradition, to a more fixed, written, literary tradition; and 2, it marks the gospel's first major cross-cultural leap: from its origins as a sub-group within Judaism to an independent religion, appealing to those beyond the confines of its original setting.

When: Scholars date the gospel between 50 and 75 CE. Most contemporary Bible scholars believe Mark was the first gospel. Some scholars of ancient papyri lean toward the earlier date, while others place its writing at or shortly after the destruction of Jerusalem's Temple in 70 CE.

Where: The exact location of Mark's writing is unknown. Mark's association with Peter and the presence of Latin loan words in the original text possibly point to Rome as its place of composition.

Why: Mark writes, in part, to fix the form of the Christian proclamation. By putting Jesus's words and actions in a narrative framework, Mark created a pattern that Matthew and Luke at least shared. Mark's account becomes the fixed standard by which the authenticity of later accounts of Jesus' life will be judged.

The Gospel
According to Mark

The Beginning
Mark 1:1 *initium evangelii Iesu Christi Filii Dei*

The[1] beginning of *the* good news of Jesus Christ, God's Son.

1:2 *sicut scriptum est in Esaia propheta ecce mitto angelum meum ante faciem tuam qui praeparabit viam tuam*

As is written in Isaiah *the* prophet, "Look, I send My angel before your face, who will prepare your way[2] –

1:3 *vox clamantis in deserto parate viam Domini rectas facite semitas eius*

"*a* voice shouting in *the* desert: get *the* Lord's road ready! Make his streets straight!"[3]

John's Ministry
1:4 *fuit Iohannes in deserto baptizans et praedicans baptismum paenitentiae in remissionem peccatorum*

John was in *the* desert, baptizing and preaching *a* baptism of repentance to sins' remission.

1:5 *et egrediebatur ad illum omnis Iudaeae regio et Hierosolymitae universi et baptizabantur ab illo in Iordane flumine confitentes peccata sua*

And all Judea's region went out to him, and all *the* Jerusalemites. And they were baptized by him in *the* Jordan river, confessing their sins.

1:6 *et erat Iohannes vestitus pilis cameli et zona pellicia circa lumbos eius et lucustas et mel silvestre edebat*

---

[1] Italicized words are those added to the English text to make better sense of the translation, yet absent in the original language. Latin, for instance, lacks definite and indefinite articles: *a*, *an*, and *the*.

[2] Malachi 3:1.

[3] Isaiah 40:3.

And John was dressed in camel hair and *a* leather belt around his privates, and he ate locusts and wild honey.

1:7 *et praedicabat dicens venit fortior me post me cuius non sum dignus procumbens solvere corrigiam calciamentorum eius*

And he preached saying, "Mightier-than-me comes after me, to whom I am not worthy, bending down, to untie his sandal lace.

1:8 *ego baptizavi vos aqua ille vero baptizabit vos Spiritu Sancto*

"I baptized you by water. He indeed will baptize you by Holy Spirit."

Jesus's Baptism
1:9 *et factum est in diebus illis venit Iesus a Nazareth Galilaeae et baptizatus est in Iordane ab Iohanne*

And it happened in those days Jesus came from Galilean Nazareth, and was baptized in *the* Jordan by John.

1:10 *et statim ascendens de aqua vidit apertos caelos et Spiritum tamquam columbam descendentem et manentem in ipso*

And immediately, going up from *the* water, he saw skies open and Spirit, like *a* dove, coming down and staying in him.

1:11 *et vox facta est de caelis tu es Filius meus dilectus in te conplacui*

And *a* voice came from *the* skies, "You are my beloved Son. I have been pleased in you."

Temptation
1:12 *et statim Spiritus expellit eum in desertum*

And immediately Spirit drives him to *the* desert.

1:13 *et erat in deserto quadraginta diebus et*

quadraginta noctibus et temptabatur a Satana eratque cum bestiis et angeli ministrabant illi

And he was in *the* desert forty days and forty nights, and he was tested by Satan, and he was with beasts, and angels ministered to him

Jesus Begins to Preach

1:14 *postquam autem traditus est Iohannes venit Iesus in Galilaeam praedicans evangelium regni Dei*

But after John was handed over, Jesus comes to Galilee, preaching good news of God's kingdom,

1:15 *et dicens quoniam impletum est tempus et adpropinquavit regnum Dei paenitemini et credite evangelio*

and saying that, "*The* time is completed, and God's kingdom has come near. Repent, and believe good news!"

Jesus Calls Disciples

1:16 *et praeteriens secus mare Galilaeae vidit Simonem et Andream fratrem eius mittentes retia in mare erant enim piscatores*

And passing by along Galilee's sea, he saw Simon and Andrew his brother throwing nets into *the* sea, for they were fishermen.

1:17 *et dixit eis Iesus venite post me et faciam vos fieri piscatores hominum*

And Jesus said to them, "Come after me, and I will make you be fishers of men."

1:18 *et protinus relictis retibus secuti sunt eum*

And leaving their nets at once, they followed him.

1:19 *et progressus inde pusillum vidit Iacobum Zebedaei et Iohannem fratrem eius et ipsos in navi conponentes retia*

And going on from there *a* little, he saw Jacob[4] of Zebedee and John his brother, and them in boats, mending nets.

1:20 *et statim vocavit illos et relicto patre suo Zebedaeo in navi cum mercennariis secuti sunt eum*

And immediately he called them and, leaving their father Zebedee in *the* boat with *the* hired help, they followed him.

Power Over Unclean Spirit
1:21 *et ingrediuntur Capharnaum et statim sabbatis ingressus synagogam docebat eos*

And they went into Capernaum. And immediately on *the* Sabbaths, going into *the* synagogue,[5] he taught them.

1:22 *et stupebant super doctrina eius erat enim docens eos quasi potestatem habens et non sicut scribae*

And they were astounded over his teaching, for he was teaching them like *one* having power, and not like *the* writers.

1:23 *et erat in synagoga eorum homo in spiritu inmundo et exclamavit*

And *a* man was in their synagogue in *an* unclean spirit. And he cried out,

1:24 *dicens quid nobis et tibi Iesu Nazarene venisti perdere nos scio qui sis Sanctus Dei*

saying, "What to us and to you, Jesus Nazarene? Have you come to destroy us? I

---

[4] AV reads "James."

[5] A synagogue is the local gathering of Jews for worship, teaching, community, and service. The name derives from the Greek word, συναγωγή which originally meant "bringing together," or "gathering." In time, the word came to designate the place of gathering, as well as the community that gathered within it. The synagogue is the model for later churches and mosques.

know who you may be – God's Holy *one*."

1:25 *et comminatus est ei Iesus dicens obmutesce et exi de homine*

And Jesus threatened him saying, "Be quiet, and come out of *the* man!"

1:26 *et discerpens eum spiritus inmundus et exclamans voce magna exivit ab eo*

And *the* unclean spirit, tearing him and shouting in *a* great voice, went out of him.

1:27 *et mirati sunt omnes ita ut conquirerent inter se dicentes quidnam est hoc quae doctrina haec nova quia in potestate et spiritibus inmundis imperat et oboediunt ei*

And all were amazed, so that they sought out among themselves, saying, "What is this? What is this new teaching, for he commands

even unclean spirits in power, and they obey him!"

1:28 *et processit rumor eius statim in omnem regionem Galilaeae*

And his reputation went out at once to all Galilee's region.

Power Over Fever
1:29 *et protinus egredientes de synagoga venerunt in domum Simonis et Andreae cum Iacobo et Iohanne*

And at once going out of *the* synagogue, they came to Simon and Andrew's house with Jacob and John.

1:30 *decumbebat autem socrus Simonis febricitans et statim dicunt ei de illa*

But Simon's mother-in-law lay down fevering, and immediately they tell him about her.

1:31 *et accedens elevavit eam adprehensa manu eius et continuo dimisit eam febris et* *ministrabat eis*

And coming near he lifted her up, taking her hand. And just then *the* fever released her, and she ministered to them.

1:32 *vespere autem facto cum occidisset sol adferebant ad eum omnes male habentes et daemonia habentes*

But evening *having* come, when *the* sun set,[6] they carried to him all having harm and having demons,

1:33 *et erat omnis civitas congregata ad ianuam*

and all *the* city was gathered at *the* door.

1:34 *et curavit multos qui vexabantur variis languoribus et daemonia multa eiciebat et non sinebat loqui ea quoniam sciebant eum*

---

[6] The Sabbath ends at sunset. The people could not lawfully come to Jesus until the Sabbath was over.

And he cared for many who were afflicted by various weaknesses, and he threw out many demons, and he didn't allow them to speak because they knew him.

1:35 *et diluculo valde surgens egressus abiit in desertum locum ibique orabat*

And getting up very early, going out, he went into *a* desert place, and he prayed there.

Simon and Others Pursue
1:36 *et persecutus est eum Simon et qui cum illo erant*

And Simon pursued him, and *those* who were with him.

1:37 *et cum invenissent eum dixerunt ei quia omnes quaerunt te*

And when they had found him, they said to him that, "Everyone is looking for you."

1:38 *et ait illis eamus in proximos vicos et civitates ut* *et ibi praedicem ad hoc enim veni*

And he said to them, "Let's go to *the* next towns and cities, so I can preach there too – for I came to *do* this."

1:39 *et erat praedicans in synagogis eorum et omni Galilaea et daemonia eiciens*

And he was preaching in their synagogues too in all Galilee, and throwing out demons.

Power Over Wasting Illness
1:40 *et venit ad eum leprosus deprecans eum et genu flexo dixit si vis potes me mundare*

And *a* leper comes to him, begging him, and, knee bent, he said, "If you want, you can make me clean."

1:41 *Iesus autem misertus eius extendit manum suam et tangens eum ait illi volo mundare*

But Jesus, pitying him, stretches out his hand and,

touching him, said to him, "I want. Be clean!"

1:42 *et cum dixisset statim discessit ab eo lepra et mundatus est*

And when he had spoken, *the* leprosy immediately withdrew from him, and he was cleansed.

1:43 *et comminatus ei statim eiecit illum*

And threatening him immediately, he threw him out.

1:44 *et dicit ei vide nemini dixeris sed vade ostende te principi sacerdotum et offer pro emundatione tua quae praecepit Moses in testimonium illis*

And he says to him, "Look, say nothing, but go show yourself to *the* priests' prince, and give for your cleansing what Moses commanded in his testimony."

1:45 *at ille egressus coepit praedicare et diffamare sermonem ita ut iam non posset manifeste in civitatem introire sed foris in desertis locis esse et conveniebant ad eum undique*

And he, going out, begins to preach and spread *the* word, so that he no longer could go openly into *a* city, but *had* to be outside in *a* desert place. And they came to him from everywhere.

The Power of Forgiveness
Mark 2:1 *et iterum intravit Capharnaum post dies*

And again after several days, he went into Capernaum.

2:2 *et auditum est quod in domo esset et convenerunt multi ita ut non caperet neque ad ianuam et loquebatur eis verbum*

And *it* was heard that he was in *the* house, and many came together, so that it couldn't hold *them*, not even at *the* door. And he spoke *a* word to them.

2:3 *et venerunt ferentes ad eum paralyticum qui a quattuor portabatur*

And they came, bringing *a* paralytic to him who was carried by four.

2:4 *et cum non possent offerre eum illi prae turba nudaverunt tectum ubi erat et patefacientes submiserunt grabattum in quo paralyticus* *iacebat*

And when they couldn't offer him to him because of *the* crowd, they stripped off *the* roof where he was. And, opening *it,* they lowered *the* cot on which *the* paralytic was placed.

2:5 *cum vidisset autem Iesus fidem illorum ait paralytico fili dimittuntur tibi peccata*

But when Jesus had seen their faith, he said to *the* paralytic, "My son, sins are forgiven you."

2:6 *erant autem illic quidam de scribis sedentes et cogitantes in cordibus suis*

But some were sitting there from *the* writers, and thinking in their hearts,

2:7 *quid hic sic loquitur blasphemat quis potest dimittere peccata nisi solus Deus*

"Why does this *man* speak so?

He blasphemes. Who can forgive sins except God alone?"

2:8 *quo statim cognito Iesus spiritu suo quia sic cogitarent intra se dicit illis quid ista cogitatis in cordibus vestris*

Jesus, knowing at once by his spirit that they thought so among themselves, said to them, "Why do you think this in your hearts?

2:9 *quid est facilius dicere paralytico dimittuntur tibi peccata an dicere surge et tolle grabattum tuum et ambula*

"What is easier: to say to *the* paralytic, 'Sins are forgiven you,' or to say, 'Get up, and take your cot, and walk?'

2:10 *ut autem sciatis quia potestatem habet Filius hominis in terra dimittendi peccata ait paralytico*

"But so you can know that man's Son has power on earth

to forgive sins," he said to *the* paralytic,

2:11 *tibi dico surge tolle grabattum tuum et vade in domum tuam*

"I say to you, get up, take your cot, and go to your house."

2:12 *et statim ille surrexit et sublato grabatto abiit coram omnibus ita ut admirarentur omnes et honorificarent Deum dicentes quia numquam sic vidimus*

And at once he got up and, taking *the* cot, went out before all, so that all were stunned. And they honored God, saying that, "We've never seen such."

Power Over Wrong Living
2:13 *et egressus est rursus ad mare omnisque turba veniebat ad eum et docebat eos*

And he went out again to *the* sea, and all *the* crowd came to him, and he taught them.

2:14 *et cum praeteriret vidit*

Levin Alphei sedentem ad teloneum et ait illi sequere me et surgens secutus est eum

And when he passed by, he saw Levi of Alphaeus sitting at *the* tax booth. And he said to him, "Follow me!" And, getting up, he followed him.

2:15 *et factum est cum accumberet in domo illius multi publicani et peccatores simul discumbebant cum Iesu et discipulis eius erant enim multi qui et sequebantur eum*

And it happened when he reclined in his house, many tax contractors and sinners reclined together with Jesus and his disciples, for *there* were many also who followed him.

2:16 *et scribae et Pharisaei videntes quia manducaret cum peccatoribus et publicanis dicebant discipulis eius quare cum publicanis et peccatoribus manducat et bibit magister vester*

And *the* writers and *the* Pharisees, seeing that he ate with sinners and tax contractors, said to his disciples, "Why does your teacher eat and drink with tax contractors and sinners?"

2:17 *hoc audito Iesus ait illis non necesse habent sani medicum sed qui male habent non enim veni vocare iustos sed peccatores*

Jesus, hearing this, said to them, "*The* healthy don't need *a* doctor, but whose who have harm – for I've not come to call *the* fair but sinners."

Power Over False Piety

2:18 *et erant discipuli Iohannis et Pharisaei ieiunantes et veniunt et dicunt illi cur discipuli Iohannis et Pharisaeorum ieiunant tui autem discipuli non ieiunant*

And John's disciples and *the* Pharisees were fasting. And they come and say to him, "Why are John's disciples and *the* Pharisees fasting, but your disciples aren't fasting?"

2:19 *et ait illis Iesus numquid possunt filii nuptiarum quamdiu sponsus cum illis est ieiunare quanto tempore habent secum sponsum non possunt ieiunare*

And Jesus said to them, "*The* wedding's sons can't fast while *the* groom is with them, can they? However long they have *the* groom with them, they can't fast.

2:20 *venient autem dies cum auferetur ab eis sponsus et tunc ieiunabunt in illa die*

"But days will come when *the* groom will be taken away from them, and then they will fast – on that day.

2:21 *nemo adsumentum panni rudis adsuit vestimento veteri alioquin aufert supplementum novum a veteri et maior scissura fit*

"No one, taking uncut cloth, sews it to *an* old shirt.

Otherwise, *the* new patch pulls away from *the* old, and *a* worse tear happens.

2:22 *et nemo mittit vinum novellum in utres veteres alioquin disrumpet vinum utres et vinum effunditur et utres peribunt sed vinum novum in utres novos mitti debet*

"And no one puts new wine in old skins. Otherwise, *the* wine bursts *the* skins, and *the* wine is spilled, and *the* skins are ruined. Yet new wine must be put into new skins."

Power Over Unreasonable Legalism

2:23 *et factum est iterum cum sabbatis ambularet per sata et discipuli eius coeperunt praegredi et vellere spicas*

And again it happened, when he was walking through *a* grain field on *the* Sabbath, and his disciples began to go before and pluck heads *of grain*.

2:24 *Pharisaei autem dicebant ei ecce quid faciunt sabbatis quod non licet*

But *the* Pharisees said to him, "Look, why are they doing what isn't legal on *the* Sabbath?"

2:25 *et ait illis numquam legistis quid fecerit David quando necessitatem habuit et esuriit ipse et qui cum eo erant*

And he said to them, "Have you never read what David did when he was in need and hungry, he and those who were with him –

2:26 *quomodo introiit in domum Dei sub Abiathar principe sacerdotum et panes propositionis manducavit quos non licet manducare nisi sacerdotibus et dedit eis qui cum eo erant*

"how he went into God's house under Abiathar, *the* priests' prince, and ate *the* loaves of propositions, which is not legal to eat except for priests? And he gave to those who were with him."

2:27 *et dicebat eis sabbatum propter hominem factum est et non homo propter sabbatum*

And he said to them, "*The* Sabbath was made for man's sake, not man for *the* Sabbath's sake.

2:28 *itaque dominus est Filius hominis etiam sabbati*

"So also man's Son is Lord even of *the* Sabbath."

Power Over What Has Dried Up

Mark 3:1 *et introivit iterum synagogam et erat ibi homo habens manum aridam*

And again he went into *a* synagogue, and *a* man having *a* dried-up hand was there.

3:2 *et observabant eum si sabbatis curaret ut accusarent illum*

And they watched him, whether he would heal on *a* Sabbath, so they could accuse him.

3:3 *et ait homini habenti manum aridam surge in medium*

And he said to *the* man having *the* dried-up hand, "Stand up in *the* middle."

3:4 *et dicit eis licet sabbatis bene facere an male animam salvam facere an perdere at illi tacebant*

And he says to them, "Is it

legal on *the* Sabbath to do well or harm, to save *a* soul or destroy it?"

And they were silent.

3:5 *et circumspiciens eos cum ira contristatus super caecitatem cordis eorum dicit homini extende manum tuam et extendit et restituta est manus illi*

And looking around at them with anger, saddened over their hearts' blindness, he says to *the* man, "Stretch out your hand."

And he stretched *it* out, and *the* hand was restored to him.

3:6 *exeuntes autem statim Pharisaei cum Herodianis consilium faciebant adversus eum quomodo eum perderent*

But going out at once, *the* Pharisees worked counsel with *the* Herodians against him, how they could destroy him.

Jesus Thronged by Multitudes

3:7 *et Iesus cum discipulis suis secessit ad mare et multa turba a Galilaea et Iudaea secuta est eum*

And Jesus with his disciples withdrew to *the* sea, and *a* large crowd followed him from Galilee and Judea,

3:8 *et ab Hierosolymis et ab Idumea et trans Iordanen et qui circa Tyrum et Sidonem multitudo magna audientes quae faciebat venerunt ad eum*

and from Jerusalem, and from Idumea, and across *the* Jordan. And those around Tyre and Sidon, *a* great multitude hearing what he did, came to him.

3:9 *et dixit discipulis suis ut navicula sibi deserviret propter turbam ne conprimerent eum*

And he told his disciples that they should prepare him *a* little boat because of *the* crowd, so they wouldn't crush him –

3:10 *multos enim sanabat ita ut inruerent in eum ut illum tangerent quotquot habebant plagas*

for he healed many, so that they rushed in to him – so as many as had sicknesses could touch him.

3:11 *et spiritus inmundi cum illum videbant procidebant ei et clamabant dicentes*

And unclean spirits, when they saw him, fell down before him and shouted, saying,

3:12 *tu es Filius Dei et vehementer comminabatur eis ne manifestarent illum*

"You are God's Son!"

And he fiercely threatened them that they not make him known.

Jesus Sets Apart
Twelve Disciples

3:13 *et ascendens in montem vocavit ad se quos voluit ipse et venerunt ad eum*

And going up onto *a* mountain, he called to him those he himself wanted, and they came to him.

3:14 *et fecit ut essent duodecim cum illo et ut mitteret eos praedicare*

And he made *it* that twelve were with him, and that he could send them to preach.

3:15 *et dedit illis potestatem curandi infirmitates et eiciendi daemonia*

And he gave them power to care for weaknesses and to throw out demons.

3:16 *et inposuit Simoni nomen Petrus*

And he placed on Simon *the* name Peter.

3:17 *et Iacobum Zebedaei et Iohannem fratrem Iacobi et inposuit eis nomina Boanerges quod est Filii tonitrui*

And on Jacob of Zebedee and John, Jacob's brother, he also placed on them *the* name Boanerges – that is, thunder's Sons.

3:18 *et Andream et Philippum et Bartholomeum et Mattheum et Thomam et Iacobum Alphei et Thaddeum et Simonem Cananeum*

And Andrew, and Philip, and Bartholomew, and Matthew, and Thomas, and Jacob of Alpheus, and Thaddeus, and Simon *the* Canaanite,

3:19 *et Iudam Scarioth qui et tradidit illum*

and Judas Scarioth, who also betrayed him.

Jesus's Enemies
Link Him to Beelzebub
3:20 *et veniunt ad domum et convenit iterum turba ita ut*

non possent neque panem manducare

And they come to *the* house, and again *a* crowd comes together so that they couldn't even eat bread.

3:21 *et cum audissent sui exierunt tenere eum dicebant enim quoniam in furorem versus est*

And when his *own* had heard, they went out to seize him, for they said that he was turned to madness.

3:22 *et scribae qui ab Hierosolymis descenderant dicebant quoniam Beelzebub habet et quia in principe daemonum eicit daemonia*

And *the* writers who had come down from Jerusalem said that, "He has Beelzebub," and that, "He throws out demons by *the* demons' prince."

3:23 *et convocatis eis in parabolis dicebat illis quomodo potest Satanas*

Satanan eicere

And calling them together, he spoke to them in comparisons, "How can Satan throw out Satan?

3:24 *et si regnum in se dividatur non potest stare regnum illud*

"And if *a* kingdom is divided in itself, that kingdom can't stand.

3:25 *et si domus super semet ipsam dispertiatur non poterit domus illa stare*

"And if *a* house is scattered over itself, that house can't stand.

3:26 *et si Satanas consurrexit in semet ipsum dispertitus est et non potest stare sed finem habet*

"And if Satan has risen against himself, he is destroyed and can't stand, but has *an* end.

3:27 *nemo potest vasa fortis*

ingressus in domum diripere nisi prius fortem alliget et tunc domum eius diripiet

"No one, going into *a* mighty one's house, can take away *the* vessels, unless he first binds *the* mighty one – and then he can plunder his house.

3:28 *amen dico vobis quoniam omnia dimittentur filiis hominum peccata et blasphemiae quibus blasphemaverint*

"Amen I say to you that all sins will be forgiven men's children, and whichever blasphemies they blaspheme.

3:29 *qui autem blasphemaverit in Spiritum Sanctum non habet remissionem in aeternum sed reus erit aeterni delicti*

"But who blasphemes in *the* Holy Spirit does not have remission in eternity, yet will be guilty of *an* eternal offense" –

3:30 *quoniam dicebant spiritum inmundum habet*

for they said, "He has *an* unclean spirit."

Power to Constitute
True Family

3:31 *et veniunt mater eius et fratres et foris stantes miserunt ad eum vocantes eum*

And his mother and brothers come and, standing outside, sent to him, calling him.

3:32 *et sedebat circa eum turba et dicunt ei ecce mater tua et fratres tui foris quaerunt te*

And he was sitting, *the* crowd around him. And they say to him, "Look, your mother and your brothers *are* outside. They are looking for you."

3:33 *et respondens eis ait quae est mater mea et fratres mei*

And answering them, he said, "Who is my mother and my brothers?"

3:34 *et circumspiciens eos qui in circuitu eius sedebant ait ecce mater mea et fratres mei*

And looking around at those who sat around him, he said, "Look, my mother and my brothers –

3:35 *qui enim fecerit voluntatem Dei hic frater meus et soror mea et mater est*

"for who does God's will, this *one* is my brother, and my sister, and mother."

Teaching By the Sea

Mark 4:1 *et iterum coepit docere ad mare et congregata est ad eum turba multa ita ut in navem ascendens sederet in mari et omnis turba circa mare super terram erat*

And again he began to teach by *the* sea and *a* great crowd gathered to him, so that, going into *a* boat, he sat on *the* sea, and all *the* crowd was on *the* land around *the* sea.

4:2 *et docebat eos in parabolis multa et dicebat illis in doctrina sua*

And he taught them in many comparisons, and he said to them in his teaching,

4:3 *audite ecce exiit seminans ad seminandum*

"Listen! Look, *a* sower went out to sow.

4:4 *et dum seminat aliud cecidit circa viam et venerunt volucres et comederunt illud*

"And while he sows, some fell along *the* path, and birds came and ate it.

4:5 *aliud vero cecidit super petrosa ubi non habuit terram multam et statim exortum est quoniam non habebat altitudinem terrae*

"Other, indeed, fell on rocky soil, where it didn't have much soil. And it sprung up quickly, because it didn't have depth of soil.

4:6 *et quando exortus est sol exaestuavit et eo quod non haberet radicem exaruit*

"And when *the* sun rose it got hot, and, because it didn't have *a* root, it dried up.

4:7 *et aliud cecidit in spinas et ascenderunt spinae et offocaverunt illud et fructum non dedit*

"And other fell among thorns, and *the* thorns grew up and choked it, and it gave no fruit.

4:8 *et aliud cecidit in terram bonam et dabat fructum ascendentem et crescentem et adferebat unum triginta et unum sexaginta et unum centum*

"And other fell in good soil and gave fruit, climbing up and growing. And one bore thirty, and one sixty, and one *a* hundred."

4:9 *et dicebat qui habet aures audiendi audiat*

And he said, "Who has ears to hear, let him hear!"

Jesus Explains His Teaching

4:10 *et cum esset singularis interrogaverunt eum hii qui cum eo erant cum duodecim parabolas*

And when he was alone, those who were with him with *the* twelve asked him *about the* comparisons.

4:11 *et dicebat eis vobis datum est mysterium regni Dei*

illis autem qui foris sunt in parabolis omnia fiunt

And he said to them, "*The* mystery of God's kingdom is given to you. But to those who are outside, all will happen by comparisons –

4:12 *ut videntes videant et non videant et audientes audiant et non intellegant nequando convertantur et dimittantur eis peccata*

"so seeing, they may see and not see. And hearing, they may hear and not understand, unless they be converted and sins be forgiven them."

4:13 *et ait illis nescitis parabolam hanc et quomodo omnes parabolas cognoscetis*

And he said to them, "Don't you understand this comparison? And how will you understand all *the* comparisons?

4:14 *qui seminat verbum seminat*

"Who sows, sows *the* word.

4:15 *hii autem sunt qui circa viam ubi seminatur verbum et cum audierint confestim venit Satanas et aufert verbum quod seminatum est in corda eorum*

"But these are *those* who are along *the* path where *the* word is sown. And as soon as they hear, Satan comes and takes away *the* word that was sown in their heart.

4:16 *et hii sunt similiter qui super petrosa seminantur qui cum audierint verbum statim cum gaudio accipiunt illud*

"And these likewise are *those* who are sown on rocky soil, who, when they hear *the* word, accept it immediately with joy.

4:17 *et non habent radicem in se sed temporales sunt deinde orta tribulatione et persecutione propter verbum confestim scandalizantur*

"And they have no root in themselves, yet are worldly.

When trouble and persecution spring up for *the* word's sake, they are scandalized at once.

4:18 *et alii sunt qui in spinis seminantur hii sunt qui verbum audiunt*

"And others are *those* who are sown among thorns. These are *those* who hear *the* word,

4:19 *et aerumnae saeculi et deceptio divitiarum et circa reliqua concupiscentiae introeuntes suffocant verbum et sine fructu efficitur*

"and *the* time's tasks, and *the* deception of riches, and lust's remaining *concerns*, entering in, suffocate *the* word, and it grows up without fruit.

4:20 *et hii sunt qui super terram bonam seminati sunt qui audiunt verbum et suscipiunt et fructificant unum triginta et unum sexaginta et unum centum*

"And these are *those* who were sown on good soil, who

hear *the* word, and receive it, and bear fruit: one thirty, and one sixty, and one *a* hundred."

Light Hidden and Made Known

4:21 *et dicebat illis numquid venit lucerna ut sub modio ponatur aut sub lecto nonne ut super candelabrum ponatur*

And he said to them, "*A* light doesn't come so it can be put under *a* bucket or under *a* bed, does it? Isn't it placed on *a* lamp stand?

4:22 *non enim est aliquid absconditum quod non manifestetur nec factum est occultum sed ut in palam veniat*

"For *there* is nothing hidden that will not be made known, nor is *anything* made hidden, yet that it may come into *the* open.

4:23 *si quis habet aures audiendi audiat*

"If one has ears to hear, let him hear!"

The Rich Get Richer

4:24 *et dicebat illis videte quid audiatis in qua mensura mensi fueritis remetietur vobis et adicietur vobis*

And he said to them, "Watch what you hear! In what measure you measure, it will be measured to you, and will be added to you.

4:25 *qui enim habet dabitur illi et qui non habet etiam quod habet auferetur ab illo*

"For who has, it will be given to him. And who does not have, even what he has will be taken away from him."

Kingdom Comparisons

4:26 *et dicebat sic est regnum Dei quemadmodum si homo iaciat sementem in terram*

And he said, "God's kingdom is like this: as if man sows seed in *the* ground.

4:27 *et dormiat et exsurgat*

nocte ac die et semen germinet et increscat dum nescit ille

"And he sleeps and gets up, night and day, and *the* seed sprouts and grows, while he does not know.

4:28 *ultro enim terra fructificat primum herbam deinde spicam deinde plenum frumentum in spica*

For *the* soil bears fruit unaided: first *the* grass, then *the* head, then *the* full grain in *the* head.

4:29 *et cum se produxerit fructus statim mittit falcem quoniam adest messis*

"And when *the* fruit has produced itself, he sends in *the* sickle at once because *the* harvest is at hand."

4:30 *et dicebat cui adsimilabimus regnum Dei aut cui parabolae conparabimus illud*

And he said, "What will we compare God's kingdom to, or what comparison will we make to it?

4:31 *sicut granum sinapis quod cum seminatum fuerit in terra minus est omnibus seminibus quae sunt in terra*

"*It is* like *a* mustard seed that, when it is sown in *the* ground, is less than all *the* seeds that are in *the* ground.

4:32 *et cum seminatum fuerit ascendit et fit maius omnibus holeribus et facit ramos magnos ita ut possint sub umbra eius aves caeli habitare*

"And when it is sown, it grows up and becomes *the* greatest of all greens. And it makes great branches, so that *the* sky's birds can make nests to live in under its shade."

4:33 *et talibus multis parabolis loquebatur eis verbum prout poterant audire*

And he spoke *the* word to them by many such

comparisons, just as they could hear.

4:34 *sine parabola autem non loquebatur eis seorsum autem discipulis suis disserebat omnia*

But he spoke nothing to them without *a* comparison. Yet apart, with his disciples, he unlocked all.

Power Over Storms
4:35 *et ait illis illa die cum sero esset factum transeamus contra*

And he said to them that day when evening had come, "Let's go across."

4:36 *et dimittentes turbam adsumunt eum ita ut erat in navi et aliae naves erant cum illo*

And, dismissing *the* crowd, they take him up so that he was in *a* boat, and other boats were with him.

4:37 *et facta est procella magna venti et fluctus mittebat in navem ita ut impleretur navis*

And *a* great wind storm came up, and *a* wave crashed into *the* boat so that it filled *the* boat.

4:38 *et erat ipse in puppi supra cervical dormiens et excitant eum et dicunt ei magister non ad te pertinet quia perimus*

And he was in *the* stern, sleeping on *a* cushion. And they wake him up and say to him, "Teacher, doesn't it pertain to you that we perish?"

4:39 *et exsurgens comminatus est vento et dixit mari tace obmutesce et cessavit ventus et facta est tranquillitas magna*

And, getting up, he threatened *the* wind and said to *the* sea, "Calm down! Be quiet!"

And *the* wind ceased and *a* great calm came about.

4:40 *et ait illis quid timidi estis necdum habetis fidem et timuerunt magno timore et dicebant ad alterutrum quis putas est iste quia et ventus et mare oboediunt ei*

And he said to them, "Why are you afraid? Don't you have faith yet?"

And they feared with *a* great fear, and said to each other, "Who do you think he is, because even wind and sea obey him?"

Power Over the Legion
Mark 5:1 *et venerunt trans fretum maris in regionem Gerasenorum*

And they went across *the* sea's strait to *the* Gerasenes' region.

5:2 *et exeunti ei de navi statim occurrit ei de monumentis homo in spiritu inmundo*

And while he was coming out of *the* boat, *a* man in *an* unclean spirit immediately met him from *the* tombs,

5:3 *qui domicilium habebat in monumentis et neque catenis iam quisquam eum poterat ligare*

who had *a* dwelling among *the* tombs, and no one could still bind him, not even with chains.

5:4 *quoniam saepe conpedibus et catenis vinctus disrupisset catenas et conpedes comminuisset et nemo poterat eum domare*

For, often bound with fetters and chains, he had broken *the* chains and smashed *the* fetters, and no one could control him.

5:5 *et semper nocte ac die in monumentis et in montibus erat clamans et concidens se lapidibus*

And always, night and day, he was shouting and cutting himself with stones, among *the* tombs and in *the* mountains.

5:6 *videns autem Iesum a longe cucurrit et adoravit eum*

But seeing Jesus from far away, he ran and worshiped him.

5:7 *et clamans voce magna dicit quid mihi et tibi Iesu Fili Dei summi adiuro te per Deum ne me torqueas*

And shouting in *a* great voice, he says, "What to me and to you, Jesus, Son of *the* highest God? I adjure you by God that you not torture me!" –

5:8 *dicebat enim illi exi spiritus inmunde ab homine*

for Jesus was saying to him, "Come out from *the* man, unclean spirit!"

5:9 *et interrogabat eum quod tibi nomen est et dicit ei Legio nomen mihi est quia multi sumus*

And *Jesus*[7] asked him, "What name is yours?"

And he says to him, "Legion is *a* name to me, because we are many."

5:10 *et deprecabatur eum multum ne se expelleret extra regionem*

And he pleaded with him much that he not be expelled outside *the* region.

5:11 *erat autem ibi circa*

---

[7] Literally, "Ane he asked him . . ."

montem grex porcorum magnus pascens

But *a* great herd of pigs was there, feeding around *the* mountain.

5:12 *et deprecabantur eum spiritus dicentes mitte nos in porcos ut in eos introeamus*

And *the* spirits pleaded with him, saying, "Send us into *the* pigs, so we can go into them!"

5:13 *et concessit eis statim Iesus et exeuntes spiritus inmundi introierunt in porcos et magno impetu grex praecipitatus est in mare ad duo milia et suffocati sunt in mare*

And Jesus conceded to them at once. And *the* unclean spirits, going out, went into *the* pigs, and *the* herd threw *itself* into *the* sea with great force – some two thousand – and they drowned in *the* sea.

5:14 *qui autem pascebant eos fugerunt et nuntiaverunt in*

civitatem et in agros et egressi sunt videre quid esset facti

But those who shepherded them ran away and told it in *the* city and in *the* fields. And they went out to see what had happened.

5:15 *et veniunt ad Iesum et vident illum qui a daemonio vexabatur sedentem vestitum et sanae mentis et timuerunt*

And they come to Jesus, and saw him who was afflicted by *the* demon sitting, clothed and with *a* sound mind. And they were afraid.

5:16 *et narraverunt illis qui viderant qualiter factum esset ei qui daemonium habuerat et de porcis*

And those who saw told them how it happened to him who had *the* demons, and about *the* pigs.

5:17 *et rogare eum coeperunt ut discederet de finibus eorum*

And they began to pray him that he leave their borders.

5:18 *cumque ascenderet navem coepit illum deprecari qui daemonio vexatus fuerat ut esset cum illo*

And when he went up into *the* boat, *the one* who was afflicted by *the* demon began to plead with him that he might be with him.

5:19 *et non admisit eum sed ait illi vade in domum tuam ad tuos et adnuntia illis quanta tibi Dominus fecerit et misertus sit tui*

And he didn't admit him, but said to him, "Go to your house, to your *people*, and tell them how much *the* Lord did for you, and He may have mercy on you!"

5:20 *et abiit et coepit praedicare in Decapoli quanta sibi fecisset Iesus et omnes mirabantur*

And he went out and began to preach in *the* Decapolis how much Jesus had done for him, and all were astounded.

Two Healings

5:21 *et cum transcendisset Iesus in navi rursus trans fretum convenit turba multa ad illum et erat circa mare*

And when Jesus had crossed *the* sea's strait again in *the* boat, *a* large crowd came together to him, and he was beside *the* sea.

5:22 *et venit quidam de archisynagogis nomine Iairus et videns eum procidit ad pedes eius*

And *a* certain *man* named Jairus, from *the* synagogue's rulers, came and, seeing him, fell at his feet.

5:23 *et deprecabatur eum multum dicens quoniam filia mea in extremis est veni inpone manus super eam ut salva sit et vivat*

And he pleaded much with

him, saying that "My daughter is at *the* end. Come! Lay hands on her, so she may be secured and live!"

5:24 *et abiit cum illo et sequebatur eum turba multa et conprimebant illum*

And he went out with him, and *the* large crowd followed him, and they pressed him.

5:25 *et mulier quae erat in profluvio sanguinis annis duodecim*

And *a* woman, who was in *a* flow of blood for twelve years,

5:26 *et fuerat multa perpessa a conpluribus medicis et erogaverat omnia sua nec quicquam profecerat sed magis deterius habebat*

and had endured much from many doctors, and had spent all she had, nor did anything help, yet she had *it* even worse —

5:27 *cum audisset de Iesu*

venit in turba retro et tetigit vestimentum eius

when she had heard of Jesus, comes behind in *the* crowd, and touched his clothing —

5:28 *dicebat enim quia si vel vestimentum eius tetigero salva ero*

for she said that "If I touch even his clothing, I will be secured."

5:29 *et confestim siccatus est fons sanguinis eius et sensit corpore quod sanata esset a plaga*

And immediately, her bloody flow dried up, and she sensed in *the* body that she was healed of *the* illness.

5:30 *et statim Iesus cognoscens in semet ipso virtutem quae exierat de eo conversus ad turbam aiebat quis tetigit vestimenta mea*

And Jesus, at once knowing in himself *the* power that had

gone out of him, turned to *the* crowd, saying, "Who touched my clothes?"

5:31 *et dicebant ei discipuli sui vides turbam conprimentem te et dicis quis me tetigit*

And his disciples said to him, "You see *the* crowd pressing you, and you say, 'Who touched me?'"

5:32 *et circumspiciebat videre eam quae hoc fecerat*

And he was looking around to see her who had done this.

5:33 *mulier autem timens et tremens sciens quod factum esset in se venit et procidit ante eum et dixit ei omnem veritatem*

But *the* woman, fearing and trembling, knowing what had happened to her, came and fell down before him, and told him *the* whole truth.

5:34 *ille autem dixit ei filia*

fides tua te salvam fecit vade in pace et esto sana a plaga tua

But he said to her, "Daughter, your faith has made you safe. Go in peace, and be healed of your sickness!"

5:35 *adhuc eo loquente veniunt ab archisynagogo dicentes quia filia tua mortua est quid ultra vexas magistrum*

While he was still speaking, they come from *the* synagogue ruler, saying that "Your daughter is dead. Why trouble *the* teacher further?"

5:36 *Iesus autem verbo quod dicebatur audito ait archisynagogo noli timere tantummodo crede*

But Jesus, hearing *the* word that they said, said to *the* synagogue ruler, "Don't be afraid! Only believe!"

5:37 *et non admisit quemquam sequi se nisi Petrum et Iacobum et*

Iohannem fratrem Iacobi

And he didn't allow anyone to follow him except Peter, and Jacob, and John, Jacob's brother.

5:38 *et veniunt in domum archisynagogi et videt tumultum et flentes et heiulantes multum*

And they come to *the* synagogue ruler's house. And he sees *the* tumult and those weeping and wailing much.

5:39 *et ingressus ait eis quid turbamini et ploratis puella non est mortua sed dormit*

And going in, he said to them, "Why are you troubled and weeping? *The* girl isn't dead, yet she sleeps."

5:40 *et inridebant eum ipse vero eiectis omnibus adsumit patrem et matrem puellae et qui secum erant et ingreditur ubi erat puella iacens*

And they mocked him. Yet he, throwing all *of them* out, took *the* girl's father and mother and those who were with him, and went in where *the* girl was laid.

5:41 *et tenens manum puellae ait illi talitha cumi quod est interpretatum puella tibi dico surge*

And, taking *the* girl's hand, he said to her, "Talitha, cumi!" (that is, interpreted, "Girl, I say to you, get up!")

5:42 *et confestim surrexit puella et ambulabat erat autem annorum duodecim et obstipuerunt stupore maximo*

And *the* girl got up at once and walked around (but she was twelve years old). And they were astounded by *the* greatest amazement.

5:43 *et praecepit illis vehementer ut nemo id sciret et dixit dari illi manducare*

And he commanded them fiercely that no one might

know it, and he said to give her *something* to eat.

Rejected at Nazareth

Mark 6:1 *et egressus inde abiit in patriam suam et sequebantur illum discipuli sui*

And going out from there, he went into his home country, and his disciples followed him.

6:2 *et facto sabbato coepit in synagoga docere et multi audientes admirabantur in doctrina eius dicentes unde huic haec omnia et quae est sapientia quae data est illi et virtutes tales quae per manus eius efficiuntur*

And, *the* Sabbath come, he began to teach in *the* synagogue. And many, hearing, admired his teaching, saying, "Where did he *get* all this, and what is *the* wisdom that was given to him, and such powers that are brought about through his hands?

6:3 *nonne iste est faber filius Mariae frater Iacobi et Ioseph et Iudae et Simonis nonne et sorores eius hic nobiscum sunt* *et scandalizabantur in illo*

"This is *the* carpenter, isn't it – Mary's son, Jacob, and Joseph, and Judah, and Simon's brother? And aren't his sisters here with us?"

And they were scandalized by him.

6:4 *et dicebat eis Iesus quia non est propheta sine honore nisi in patria sua et in cognatione sua et in domo sua*

And Jesus said to them that "*A* prophet isn't without honor except in his home country, and among his clan, and in his *own* house."

6:5 *et non poterat ibi virtutem ullam facere nisi paucos infirmos inpositis manibus curavit*

And he couldn't work any power there, except he healed *a* few sick, laying on hands.

6:6 *et mirabatur propter incredulitatem eorum*

And he was astounded at their disbelief.

Power Extended Through Disciples

6:7 *et circumibat castella in circuitu docens et convocavit duodecim et coepit eos mittere binos et dabat illis potestatem spirituum inmundorum*

And he went through *the* villages around, teaching. And he called *the* twelve together, and began to send them by twos, and gave them power over unclean spirits.

6:8 *et praecepit eis ne quid tollerent in via nisi virgam tantum non peram non panem neque in zona aes*

And he commanded them that they take nothing on *the* road except *a* staff only – not *a* bag, not bread, nor coins in *the* belt,

6:9 *sed calciatos sandaliis et ne induerentur duabus tunicis*

yet be shoed in sandals, and

they not put on two tunics.

6:10 *et dicebat eis quocumque introieritis in domum illic manete donec exeatis inde*

And he said to them, "Wherever you enter into *a* house, stay there until you leave from there.

6:11 *et quicumque non receperint vos nec audierint vos exeuntes inde excutite pulverem de pedibus vestris in testimonium illis*

"And whoever won't receive you or listen to you, shake *the* dust from your feet going out from there as *a* testimony to them."

6:12 *et exeuntes praedicabant ut paenitentiam agerent*

And, going out, they preached that *people* should act out penitence.

6:13 *et daemonia multa eiciebant et unguebant oleo*

multos aegrotos et sanabant

And they threw out many demons, and anointed many sick with oil, and healed *them.*

Power to Trouble the Powerful

6:14 *et audivit Herodes rex manifestum enim factum est nomen eius et dicebat quia Iohannes Baptista resurrexit a mortuis et propterea inoperantur virtutes in illo*

And King Herod heard, for his name was made known. And he said that "John *the* Baptist has risen from *the* dead, and for this reason powers are at work in him."

6:15 *alii autem dicebant quia Helias est alii vero dicebant propheta est quasi unus ex prophetis*

But others said that he is Elijah. Others, indeed, said he is *a* prophet like one of *the* prophets.

6:16 *quo audito Herodes ait*

quem ego decollavi Iohannem hic a mortuis resurrexit

Herod, when he heard, said, "John, whom I beheaded – he has risen from *the* dead."

6:17 *ipse enim Herodes misit ac tenuit Iohannem et vinxit eum in carcere propter Herodiadem uxorem Philippi fratris sui quia duxerat eam*

For Herod himself sent, and seized John, and bound him in prison for *the* sake of Herodias, his brother Philip's wife, because he had married her.

6:18 *dicebat enim Iohannes Herodi non licet tibi habere uxorem fratris tui*

For John said to Herod, "It isn't legal for you to have your brother's wife."

6:19 *Herodias autem insidiabatur illi et volebat occidere eum nec poterat*

But Herodias plotted against

him and wanted to kill him, yet couldn't –

6:20 *Herodes enim metuebat Iohannem sciens eum virum iustum et sanctum et custodiebat eum et audito eo multa faciebat et libenter eum audiebat*

for Herod feared John, knowing him to be *a* fair and holy man. And he kept him, and, hearing him, did many *things*. And he heard him freely.

John the Baptist's Execution
6:21 *et cum dies oportunus accidisset Herodes natalis sui cenam fecit principibus et tribunis et primis Galilaeae*

And when *an* opportune day had occurred, Herod made *a* feast on his birthday for Galilee's princes and tribunes and leading citizens.

6:22 *cumque introisset filia ipsius Herodiadis et saltasset et placuisset Herodi simulque* *recumbentibus rex ait puellae pete a me quod vis et dabo tibi*

And when Herodias's daughter had come in and danced and pleased Herod and all those reclining *at table* together, *the* king said to *the* girl, "Ask from me what you want, and I will give *it* to you."

6:23 *et iuravit illi quia quicquid petieris dabo tibi licet dimidium regni mei*

And he swore to her that "Whatever you ask I will give you, even half my kingdom."

6:24 *quae cum exisset dixit matri suae quid petam et illa dixit caput Iohannis Baptistae*

She,[8] when she had gone out, said to her mother, "What will I ask?"

And she said, "John *the* Baptist's head."

---

[8] Literally, "Who, when she had gone out . . ."

6:25 *cumque introisset statim cum festinatione ad regem petivit dicens volo ut protinus des mihi in disco caput Iohannis Baptistae*

And when she had come in at once with haste to *the* king, she asked, saying, "I want that you give me at once John *the* Baptist's head on *a* plate."

6:26 *et contristatus rex propter iusiurandum et propter simul recumbentes noluit eam contristare*

And *the* king, saddened, because of *the* oath and because of those reclining *at table* with him, didn't want to disappoint her.

6:27 *sed misso speculatore praecepit adferri caput eius in disco et decollavit eum in carcere*

Yet, sending a scout, he commanded him to bring his head on *a* plate. And he cut his head off in *the* prison.

6:28 *et adtulit caput eius in disco et dedit illud puellae et puella dedit matri suae*

And he brought his head on *a* plate, and gave it to *the* girl, and *the* girl gave *it* to her mother.

6:29 *quo audito discipuli eius venerunt et tulerunt corpus eius et posuerunt illud in monumento*

John's[9] disciples, when they heard, came and took his body, and placed it in *a* tomb.

The Missionaries Return to Jesus

6:30 *et convenientes apostoli ad Iesum renuntiaverunt illi omnia quae egerant et docuerant*

And *the* apostles,[10] coming

---

[9] Literally, "His disciples . . ."

[10] The Greek word ἀπόστολος comes from a verb meaning "to send." The disciples only become apostles when they are

together to Jesus, told him all that they had done and taught.

6:31 *et ait illis venite seorsum in desertum locum et requiescite pusillum erant enim qui veniebant et rediebant multi et nec manducandi spatium habebant*

And he said to them, "Come away to *a* deserted place and rest *a* little."

For there were many who were coming and going, and they didn't *even* have space to eat.

6:32 *et ascendentes in navi abierunt in desertum locum seorsum*

And, going up into *a* boat, they went away to *a* deserted place.

6:33 *et viderunt eos abeuntes et cognoverunt multi et pedestre et de omnibus civitatibus concurrerunt illuc et praevenerunt eos*

---

sent out to share the Good News.

And they saw them going, and many knew. And they ran together there on foot from all *the* cities, and came there before them.

Power to Feed
Hungry Seekers

6:34 *et exiens vidit multam turbam Iesus et misertus est super eos quia erant sicut oves non habentes pastorem et coepit docere illos multa*

And, going out, Jesus saw *the* large crowd and had pity on them, for they were like sheep not having *a* shepherd. And he began to teach them many *things*.

6:35 *et cum iam hora multa fieret accesserunt discipuli eius dicentes desertus est locus hic et iam hora praeterivit*

And when *a* late hour had already come, his disciples came to him, saying, "This is *a* deserted place and *the* hour has already passed.

6:36 *dimitte illos ut euntes in proximas villas et vicos emant sibi cibos quos manducent*

"Dismiss them so, going to *the* nearby villages and towns, they can buy themselves food which they will eat."

6:37 *et respondens ait illis date illis manducare et dixerunt ei euntes emamus denariis ducentis panes et dabimus eis manducare*

And answering, he said to them, "Give them *something* to eat!"

And they said to him, "Will we go out and buy two hundred days' worth[11] of bread, and give them *something* to eat?"

6:38 *et dicit eis quot panes habetis ite et videte et cum cognovissent dicunt quinque et duos pisces*

---

[11] A denarius, the type of money cited, was enough to buy food for a family of four for one day.

And he says to them, "How many loaves do you have? Go and see."

And when they had checked, they say, "Five, and two fish."

6:39 *et praecepit illis ut accumbere facerent omnes secundum contubernia super viride faenum*

And he commanded them that they make all sit down by companies on *the* green grass.

6:40 *et discubuerunt in partes per centenos et per quinquagenos*

And they sat down in parts, by hundreds and by fifties.[12]

6:41 *et acceptis quinque panibus et duobus piscibus intuens in caelum benedixit et fregit panes et dedit discipulis suis ut ponerent ante eos et duos pisces divisit omnibus*

---

[12] Note the quasi-military organization of the crowd.

And, taking *the* five loaves and two fish, looking to *the* sky, he blessed and broke bread, and gave *it* to his disciples, so they could put *it* in front of them. And he divided *the* two fish among all.

6:42 *et manducaverunt omnes et saturati sunt*

And all ate and were full.

6:43 *et sustulerunt reliquias fragmentorum duodecim cofinos plenos et de piscibus*

And they took up what remained – twelve baskets full of fragments and of fish.

6:44 *erant autem qui manducaverunt quinque milia virorum*

But those who ate were five thousand men.

6:45 *et statim coegit discipulos suos ascendere navem ut praecederent eum trans fretum ad Bethsaidam* *dum ipse dimitteret populum*

And at once he gathered his disciples to go up into *the* boat, so they could go before him across *the* strait to Bethsaida while he dismissed *the* people.

6:46 *et cum dimisisset eos abiit in montem orare*

And when he had dismissed them, he went out onto *the* mountain to pray.

Power Over the Sea
6:47 *et cum sero esset erat navis in medio mari et ipse solus in terra*

And when it was late, *the* boat was in *the* middle of *the* sea, and he *was* alone on *the* land.

6:48 *et videns eos laborantes in remigando erat enim ventus contrarius eis et circa quartam vigiliam noctis venit ad eos ambulans super mare et volebat praeterire eos*

And, seeing them working

hard in rowing – for *the* wind was against them – and around *the* fourth watch of *the* night, he came to them, walking on *the* sea. And he wanted to pass them by.[13]

6:49 *at illi ut viderunt eum ambulantem super mare putaverunt fantasma esse et exclamaverunt*

And they, as they saw him walking on *the* sea, considered him to be *a* ghost, and they cried out –

6:50 *omnes enim eum viderunt et conturbati sunt et statim locutus est cum eis et dixit illis confidite ego sum nolite timere*

for all saw him and were troubled. And immediately he spoke with them, and said to them, "Be faithful! I am.

---

[13] Compare Exodus 33:22: ". . . and when My glory passes by, I will put you in *the* rock's opening and protect you by My right hand until I pass by."

Don't be afraid!"

6:51 *et ascendit ad illos in navem et cessavit ventus et plus magis intra se stupebant*

And he went up to them in *the* boat, and *the* wind ceased, and they were astounded even more among themselves –

6:52 *non enim intellexerant de panibus erat enim cor illorum obcaecatum*

for they had not understood about *the* loaves,[14] for their heart was blinded.

Landing at Gennesareth
6:53 *et cum transfretassent pervenerunt in terram Gennesareth et adplicuerunt*

And when they had crossed over, they came through to Gennesareth land and put ashore.

---

[14] See Exodus 16. God alone is able to supply bread from heaven.

6:54 *cumque egressi essent de navi continuo cognoverunt eum*

And when they came out of *the* boat, they recognized him at once.

6:55 *et percurrentes universam regionem illam coeperunt in grabattis eos qui se male habebant circumferre ubi audiebant eum esse*

And, running through all that region, they began to bring on cots those who had harms, wherever they heard him to be.

6:56 *et quocumque introibat in vicos vel in villas aut civitates in plateis ponebant infirmos et deprecabantur eum ut vel fimbriam vestimenti eius tangerent et quotquot tangebant eum salvi fiebant*

And wherever he entered, in towns or in villages or in cities, they put *the* sick in *the* streets and begged him that they might touch *the* fringe of his clothing. And as many as touched him were made whole.

What Is Unclean?

Mark 7:1 *et conveniunt ad eum Pharisaei et quidam de scribis venientes ab Hierosolymis*

And *the* Pharisees and some of *the* writers come together to him, coming from Jerusalem.

7:2 *et cum vidissent quosdam ex discipulis eius communibus manibus id est non lotis manducare panes vituperaverunt*

And when they had seen some of his disciples eating bread with common hands – that is, not washed – they disrespected *him* –

7:3 *Pharisaei enim et omnes Iudaei nisi crebro lavent manus non manducant tenentes traditionem seniorum*

for *the* Pharisees and all *the* Jews do not eat unless they frequently wash hands, holding to *the* elders' tradition.

7:4 *et a foro nisi baptizentur non comedunt et alia multa sunt quae tradita sunt illis servare baptismata calicum et urceorum et aeramentorum et lectorum*

And they do not eat *foods* from outside, unless they are immersed, and *there* are many other practices that are handed down to them – to observe washings of cups, and pitchers, and copper pots, and beds.

7:5 *et interrogant eum Pharisaei et scribae quare discipuli tui non ambulant iuxta traditionem seniorum sed communibus manibus manducant panem*

And *the* Pharisees and writers asked him, "Why don't your disciples walk according to *the* elders' tradition, yet they eat bread with common hands?"

7:6 *at ille respondens dixit eis bene prophetavit Esaias de vobis hypocritis sicut scriptum est populus hic labiis me honorat cor autem eorum longe est a me*

And he, answering, said to them, "Isaiah prophesied well about you hypocrites, as is written: 'This people honors Me with lips, but their heart is far from Me.'[15]

7:7 *in vanum autem me colunt docentes doctrinas praecepta hominum*

"But they worship Me in vain, teaching *as* doctrines human commandments.

7:8 *relinquentes enim mandatum Dei tenetis traditionem hominum baptismata urceorum et calicum et alia similia his facitis multa*

"For, letting go God's commandment, you hold on to human tradition: *the* washings of pitchers and cups. And you do many other similar *things*."

---

[15] Isaiah 29:13.

7:9 *et dicebat illis bene irritum facitis praeceptum Dei ut traditionem vestram servetis*

And he said to them, "You make God's commandment well void so you can serve your tradition –

7:10 *Moses enim dixit honora patrem tuum et matrem tuam et qui maledixerit patri aut matri morte moriatur*

"for Moses said, 'Honor your father and your mother,'[16] and, 'Let who curses father or mother die by execution.'[17]

7:11 *vos autem dicitis si dixerit homo patri aut matri corban quod est donum quodcumque ex me tibi profuerit*

"But you say if *a* man says to

father or mother, 'Whatever gift from me would have benefitted you, that is Corban'[18] –

7:12 *et ultra non dimittitis eum quicquam facere patri suo aut matri*

"and you do not allow him to do anything more for his father or mother,

7:13 *rescindentes verbum Dei per traditionem vestram quam tradidistis et similia huiusmodi multa facitis*

"annulling God's word through your tradition which you handed on. And you do many similar *things*."

7:14 *et advocans iterum turbam dicebat illis audite me omnes et intellegite*

And calling *the* crowd together again, he said to them, "Listen to me, all *of you,* and

---

[16] Exodus 20:12; Deuteronomy 5:16.

[17] Exodus 21:17; Leviticus 20:9.

---

[18] *Corban* means "a gift offered to God."

understand!

7:15 *nihil est extra hominem introiens in eum quod possit eum coinquinare sed quae de homine procedunt illa sunt quae communicant hominem*

"Nothing is outside *a* man that, going into him, can make him unclean. But what comes out of *a* man, those are what make *a* man unclean.

7:16 *si quis habet aures audiendi audiat*

"If one has ears to hear, let him hear!"

Jesus Explains the Teaching
7:17 *et cum introisset in domum a turba interrogabant eum discipuli eius parabolam*

And when he had gone into *a* house away from *the* crowd, his disciples asked him about *the* comparison.

7:18 *et ait illis sic et vos inprudentes estis non intellegitis quia omne*

extrinsecus introiens in hominem non potest eum communicare

And he said to them, "So, are you imprudent too? Don't you understand that nothing external going into *a* man can make him unclean,

7:19 *quia non introit in cor eius sed in ventrem et in secessum exit purgans omnes escas*

"because it doesn't go into his heart, but into *the* gut. And it goes out into *the* waste, purging all foods."

7:20 *dicebat autem quoniam quae de homine exeunt illa communicant hominem*

But he said that, "What comes out of *a* man makes *a* man unclean –

7:21 *ab intus enim de corde hominum cogitationes malae procedunt adulteria fornicationes homicidia* "for from inside, from man's heart, harmful thoughts come out: adulteries, fornications, murders,

7:22 *furta avaritiae nequitiae dolus inpudicitia oculus malus blasphemia superbia stultitia*

"thefts, greed, worthlessness, deceit, sexual impurity, *an* evil eye, blasphemy, pride, foolishness.

7:23 *omnia haec mala ab intus procedunt et communicant hominem*

"All these harms come out from inside, and they make *a* man unclean."

Power to Heal
Even Outsiders

7:24 *et inde surgens abiit in fines Tyri et Sidonis et ingressus domum neminem voluit scire et non potuit latere*

And going up from there, he went into *the* borders of Tyre and Sidon. And, going into *a* house, he wanted no one to know, yet he couldn't be hidden.

7:25 *mulier enim statim ut audivit de eo cuius habebat filia spiritum inmundum intravit et procidit ad pedes eius*

For *a* woman whose daughter had *an* unclean spirit, as soon as she heard about him, came in and threw herself down at his feet.

7:26 *erat autem mulier gentilis Syrophoenissa genere et rogabat eum ut daemonium eiceret de filia eius*

But *the* woman was *a* gentile, of Syrophoenican nationality, and she pleaded with him that he throw *the* demon out of her daughter.

7:27 *qui dixit illi sine prius saturari filios non est enim bonum sumere panem filiorum et mittere canibus*

He[19] said to her, "Unless *the* sons are filled first, it isn't good to take *the* children's bread and throw it to dogs."

7:28 *at illa respondit et dicit ei utique Domine nam et catelli sub mensa comedunt de micis puerorum*

And she answered him and says to him, "Of course, Lord. Yet even *the* puppies under *the* table eat from *the* boys' crumbs."

7:29 *et ait illi propter hunc sermonem vade exiit daemonium de filia tua*

And he said to her, "Because of this word, go. *The* demon has gone out of your daughter."

7:30 *et cum abisset domum suam invenit puellam iacentem supra lectum et daemonium exisse*

And when she had come to her house, she found *the* girl lying on *the* bed, and *the* demon gone out.

Power to Release Those Imprisoned Within Themselves

7:31 *et iterum exiens de finibus Tyri venit per Sidonem ad mare Galilaeae inter medios fines Decapoleos*

And going out again from Tyre's borders, he came through Sidon to Galilee's Sea, into *the* middle of *the* Decapolis's borders.

7:32 *et adducunt ei surdum et mutum et deprecantur eum ut inponat illi manum*

And they bring him *a* deaf and mute, and they plead with him that he lay hands on him.

7:33 *et adprehendens eum de turba seorsum misit digitos suos in auriculas et expuens tetigit linguam eius*

And, taking him apart from

the crowd, he put his fingers in *his* ears. And, spitting, he touched his tongue.

7:34 *et suspiciens in caelum ingemuit et ait illi eppheta quod est adaperire*

And looking up into the sky, he groaned and said to him, "Ep-pheta," which is, "Be opened!"

7:35 *et statim apertae sunt aures eius et solutum est vinculum linguae eius et loquebatur recte*

And his ears were opened at once, and his tongue's chain was broken, and he spoke rightly.

7:36 *et praecepit illis ne cui dicerent quanto autem eis praecipiebat tanto magis plus praedicabant*

And he commanded them that they not tell *it* to anyone, but *the* more he commanded, *the* more they preached *it*.

7:37 *et eo amplius admirabantur dicentes bene omnia fecit et surdos facit audire et mutos loqui*

And they were astonished even more at him, saying, "He has done all *things* well. He even makes *the* deaf hear and *the* mute speak."

**Power (Again)
To Feed the Hungry**
Mark 8:1 *in illis diebus iterum cum turba multa esset nec haberent quod manducarent convocatis discipulis ait illis*

Again in those days, when *the* crowd was large, nor did they have what they could eat, calling *the* disciples, *Jesus* said to them,

8:2 *misereor super turba quia ecce iam triduo sustinent me nec habent quod manducent*

"I have pity on *the* crowd because, look. Already they sustain me three days, nor do they have what they can eat.

8:3 *et si dimisero eos ieiunos in domum suam deficient in via quidam enim ex eis de longe venerunt*

"And if I send them out hungry to their houses, they will falter on *the* way – for some of them have come from far away."

8:4 *et responderunt ei discipuli sui unde istos poterit quis hic saturare panibus in solitudine*

And his disciples answered him, "Where can one fill these with bread here in *the* wasteland?

8:5 *et interrogavit eos quot panes habetis qui dixerunt septem*

And he asked them, "How many loaves do you have?"

They[20] said, "Seven.

8:6 *et praecepit turbae discumbere supra terram et accipiens septem panes gratias agens fregit et dabat discipulis suis ut adponerent et adposuerunt turbae*

And he commanded *the* crowd to sit down on *the* ground. And, taking *the* seven loaves, giving thanks, he broke *them* and gave *them* to his disciples,

---

[20] Literally, "Who said . . ."

so they give *them* out. And they placed them before *the* crowd.

8:7 *et habebant pisciculos paucos et ipsos benedixit et iussit adponi*

And they had *a* few small fish, and he blessed them, and commanded *them* to be given.

8:8 *et manducaverunt et saturati sunt et sustulerunt quod superaverat de fragmentis septem sportas*

And they ate and were full. And they took what remained from *the* fragments: seven baskets.

8:9 *erant autem qui manducaverunt quasi quattuor milia et dimisit eos*

But *those* who ate were like four thousand. And he dismissed them.

Will a Sign Be Given?
8:10 *et statim ascendens navem cum discipulis suis*

venit in partes Dalmanutha

And going up at once onto *a* boat with his disciples, he comes to Dalmanutha's portions.

8:11 *et exierunt Pharisaei et coeperunt conquirere cum eo quaerentes ab illo signum de caelo temptantes eum*

And *the* Pharisees went out and began to investigate with him, seeking from him *a* sign from *the* sky – testing him.

8:12 *et ingemescens spiritu ait quid generatio ista quaerit signum amen dico vobis si dabitur generationi isti signum*

And, groaning in spirit, he said, "Why does this generation seek *a* sign? Amen I say to you whether this generation will be given *a* sign."

8:13 *et dimittens eos ascendens iterum abiit trans fretum*

And, dismissing them, going aboard again, he went across *the* strait.

8:14 *et obliti sunt sumere panes et nisi unum panem non habebant secum in navi*

And they forgot to take bread, and had only one loaf with them in *the* boat.

The Pharisees' Leaven
8:15 *et praecipiebat eis dicens videte cavete a fermento Pharisaeorum et fermento Herodis*

And he commanded them, saying, "Look, beware of *the* Pharisees' leaven, and Herod's leaven!"

8:16 *et cogitabant ad alterutrum dicentes quia panes non habemus*

And they considered with each other, saying that "We have no bread."

8:17 *quo cognito Iesus ait illis quid cogitatis quia panes non habetis nondum cognoscitis nec intellegitis adhuc caecatum habetis cor vestrum*

Knowing this, Jesus said to them, "Why do you think that we have no bread? Don't you recognize or understand yet? Do you still have your hearts blinded?

8:18 *oculos habentes non videtis et aures habentes non auditis nec recordamini*

"Having eyes, do you not see? And having ears, do you not hear? Don't you remember

8:19 *quando quinque panes fregi in quinque milia et quot cofinos fragmentorum plenos sustulistis dicunt ei duodecim*

"when I broke five loaves among five thousand? And how many containers full of fragments did you take up?"

They say to him, "Twelve."

8:20 *quando et septem panes*

in quattuor milia quot sportas fragmentorum tulistis et dicunt ei septem

"When also seven loaves among four thousand, how many baskets did you take up?"

And they say to him, "Seven."

8:21 *et dicebat eis quomodo nondum intellegitis*

And he said to them, "How do you still not understand?"

Power Over Blindness
8:22 *et veniunt Bethsaida et adducunt ei caecum et rogabant eum ut illum tangeret*

And they come to Bethsaida, and they bring him *a* blind *man*, and plead with him that he touch him.

8:23 *et adprehendens manum caeci eduxit eum extra vicum et expuens in oculos eius inpositis manibus suis interrogavit eum si aliquid*

videret

And, taking *the* blind man's hand, he led him outside *the* town. And, spitting in his eyes, laying on his hands, he asked him if he saw anything.

8:24 *et aspiciens ait video homines velut arbores ambulantes*

And looking, he said, "I see men like trees walking."

8:25 *deinde iterum inposuit manus super oculos eius et coepit videre et restitutus est ita ut videret clare omnia*

Then again he laid hands on his eyes, and he began to see and was restored, so that he could see all clearly.

8:26 *et misit illum in domum suam dicens vade in domum tuam et si in vicum introieris nemini dixeris*

And he sent him to his house, saying, "Go to your house and, if you go into town, you will tell no one."

Who Am I?
8:27 *et egressus est Iesus et discipuli eius in castella Caesareae Philippi et in via interrogabat discipulos suos dicens eis quem me dicunt esse homines*

And Jesus went out, and his disciples, to *the* strongholds of Caesarea Philippi. And he asked his disciples on *the* way, saying to them, "Whom do men say me to be?"

8:28 *qui responderunt illi dicentes Iohannem Baptistam alii Heliam alii vero quasi unum de prophetis*

They[21] answered him, "John *the* Baptist, others Elijah, and others like one of *the* prophets."

8:29 *tunc dicit illis vos vero quem me dicitis esse respondens Petrus ait ei tu es*

---

[21] Literally, "Who answered him . . ."

Christus

Then he says to them, "But you, whom do you say me to be?"

Peter, answering, said to him, "You are Christ."

8:30 *et comminatus est eis ne cui dicerent de illo*

And he threatened them that they say nothing to *anyone* about him.

Jesus First Predicts His Death and Resurrection
8:31 *et coepit docere illos quoniam oportet Filium hominis multa pati et reprobari a senioribus et a summis sacerdotibus et scribis et occidi et post tres dies resurgere*

And he began to teach them that man's Son must suffer much, and be rejected by *the* elders and *the* high priests and *the* writers – and be killed and, after three days, rise again.

8:32 *et palam verbum loquebatur et adprehendens eum Petrus coepit increpare eum*

And *the* word was spoken openly and Peter, taking him, began to rebuke him.

8:33 *qui conversus et videns discipulos suos comminatus est Petro dicens vade retro me Satana quoniam non sapis quae Dei sunt sed quae sunt hominum*

Jesus,[22] turning and seeing his disciples, threatened Peter, saying, "Go behind me, Satan, because you aren't tasting what are God's, but what are men's."

8:34 *et convocata turba cum discipulis suis dixit eis si quis vult post me sequi deneget se ipsum et tollat crucem suam et sequatur me*

And, calling together *the*

---

[22] Literally, "Who, turning and seeing . . ."

crowd with his disciples, he said to them, "If someone wants to follow after me, let him deny himself, and take up his cross, and follow me –

8:35 *qui enim voluerit animam suam salvam facere perdet eam qui autem perdiderit animam suam propter me et evangelium salvam eam faciet*

"for who wants to make his soul safe will lose it, but who loses his soul for my sake and *the* gospel's will make it safe.

8:36 *quid enim proderit homini si lucretur mundum totum et detrimentum faciat animae suae*

"For what does it benefit man if he makes *a* profit from *the* whole world, yet works harm to his soul?

8:37 *aut quid dabit homo commutationem pro anima sua*

"Or what will man given in exchange for his soul?

8:38 *qui enim me confusus fuerit et mea verba in generatione ista adultera et peccatrice et Filius hominis confundetur eum cum venerit in gloria Patris sui cum angelis sanctis*

"For who will be upset by me and my word in this adulterous and sinful generation, man's Son will be upset by him when he comes in *the* Father's glory with *the* holy angels.

8:39 *et dicebat illis amen dico vobis quia sunt quidam de hic stantibus qui non gustabunt mortem donec videant regnum Dei veniens in virtute*

And he said to them, "Amen I say to you that some are standing here who will not taste death until they see God's kingdom coming in power."

Jesus Transfigured

Mark 9:1 *et post dies sex adsumit Iesus Petrum et Iacobum et Iohannem et ducit illos in montem excelsum seorsum solos et transfiguratus est coram ipsis*

And after six days, Jesus took Peter, and Jacob, and John, and led them apart onto *a* high mountain alone. And he was transfigured before them.

9:2 *et vestimenta eius facta sunt splendentia candida nimis velut nix qualia fullo super terram non potest candida facere*

And his clothes became radiant, overwhelmingly white like snow, what sort no cloth dyer on earth can make white.

9:3 *et apparuit illis Helias cum Mose et erant loquentes cum Iesu*

And Elijah appeared to him with Moses, and they were speaking with Jesus.

9:4 *et respondens Petrus ait Iesu rabbi bonum est hic nos esse et faciamus tria tabernacula tibi unum et Mosi unum et Heliae unum*

And Peter, answering, said to Jesus, "Rabbi, *it* is good for us to be here – and let us make three tents: one for you, and one for Moses, and one for Elijah" –

9:5 *non enim sciebat quid diceret erant enim timore exterriti*

for he didn't know what he should say, for they were terrified by fear.

9:6 *et facta est nubes obumbrans eos et venit vox de nube dicens hic est Filius meus carissimus audite illum*

And *a* cloud came, overshadowing them. And *a* voice comes from *the* cloud, saying, "This is my Son, most beloved. Listen to him!"

9:7 *et statim circumspicientes*

neminem amplius viderunt nisi Iesum tantum secum

And looking around at once, they saw no one further with them except Jesus alone.

The Disciples
Struggle to Understand
9:8 *et descendentibus illis de monte praecepit illis ne cui quae vidissent narrarent nisi cum Filius hominis a mortuis resurrexerit*

And while they climbed down from *the* mountain, he commanded them that they not tell anyone what they had seen, except when man's Son should rise from *the* dead.

9:9 *et verbum continuerunt apud se conquirentes quid esset cum a mortuis resurrexerit*

And they kept *the* word with them, asking together what was, "When he should rise from *the* dead."

9:10 *et interrogabant eum*

dicentes quid ergo dicunt Pharisaei et scribae quia Heliam oporteat venire primum

And they asked him, saying, "Why, then, do *the* Pharisees and writers say that Elijah must come first?"

9:11 *qui respondens ait illis Helias cum venerit primo restituet omnia et quomodo scriptum est in Filium hominis ut multa patiatur et contemnatur*

Jesus,[23] answering, said to them, "Elijah, when he comes first, will restore all. And how is it written about man's Son that he may suffer many things and be condemned?

9:12 *sed dico vobis quia et Helias venit et fecerunt illi quaecumque voluerunt sicut scriptum est de eo*

"Yet I say to you that Elijah

---

[23] Literally, Who, answering, said . . ."

came, and they did whatever they wanted to him – as is written about him."

**The Power
of Prayer and Fasting**
9:13 *et veniens ad discipulos suos vidit turbam magnam circa eos et scribas conquirentes cum illis*

And coming to his disciples, he sees *a* great crowd around them, and *the* writers talking with them.

9:14 *et confestim omnis populus videns eum stupefactus est et adcurrentes salutabant eum*

And immediately, all *the* people seeing him were astounded. And, running together, they saluted him.

9:15 *et interrogavit eos quid inter vos conquiritis*

And he asked them, "What are you talking *about* among yourselves?"

9:16 *et respondens unus de turba dixit magister adtuli filium meum ad te habentem spiritum mutum*

And one from *the* crowd, responding, said, "Teacher, I brought my son to you, having *a* deaf spirit –

9:17 *qui ubicumque eum adprehenderit adlidit eum et spumat et stridet dentibus et arescit et dixi discipulis tuis ut eicerent illum et non potuerunt*

"who, wherever he seizes him, crushes him. And he foams, and grinds his teeth, and dries up. And I said to your disciples that they throw him out, and they couldn't."

9:18 *qui respondens eis dicit o generatio incredula quamdiu apud vos ero quamdiu vos patiar adferte illum ad me*

Jesus,[24] answering them, says, "O unbelieving generation,

---

[24] Literally, "Who, answering them . . ."

how long will I be with you? How long will I put up with you? Bring him to me!"

9:19 *et adtulerunt eum et cum vidisset illum statim spiritus conturbavit eum et elisus in terram volutabatur spumans*

And they brought him and, when he had seen him, *the* spirit immediately troubled him and, striking *him* to *the* ground, he writhed, foaming.

9:20 *et interrogavit patrem eius quantum temporis est ex quo hoc ei accidit at ille ait ab infantia*

And he asked his father, "How much time is *it* since this has happened to him?"

And he answered, "Since infancy –

9:21 *et frequenter eum et in ignem et in aquas misit ut eum perderet sed si quid potes adiuva nos misertus nostri*

"and it often throws him into

fire and into water so it can destroy him. But if you can help, have mercy on us!"

9:22 *Iesus autem ait illi si potes credere omnia possibilia credenti*

But Jesus said to him, "If you can believe, all *of these* are possible to those who believe."

9:23 *et continuo exclamans pater pueri cum lacrimis aiebat credo adiuva incredulitatem meam*

And shouting at once, *the* boy's father said with tears, "I believe. Help my unbelief!"

9:24 *et cum videret Iesus concurrentem turbam comminatus est spiritui inmundo dicens illi surde et mute spiritus ego tibi praecipio exi ab eo et amplius ne introeas in eum*

And when Jesus saw *the* crowd coming together, he threatened *the* unclean spirit,

saying to him "Deaf and dumb spirit, I command you to come out of him, and you may never go into him again!"

9:25 *et clamans et multum discerpens eum exiit ab eo et factus est sicut mortuus ita ut multi dicerent quia mortuus est*

And shouting and tearing him much, he went out of him. And he became like *the* dead, so that many said that, "He is dead."

9:26 *Iesus autem tenens manum eius elevavit illum et surrexit*

But Jesus, taking his hand, lifted him up, and he rose.

9:27 *et cum introisset in domum discipuli eius secreto interrogabant eum quare nos non potuimus eicere eum*

And when he had gone into *a* house, his disciples asked him in secret, "Why couldn't we throw him out?"

9:28 *et dixit illis hoc genus in nullo potest exire nisi in oratione et ieiunio*

And he said to them, "This kind can go out in no way, except by prayer and fasting."

A Second Prediction of Rejection and Death

9:29 *et inde profecti praetergrediebantur Galilaeam nec volebat quemquam scire*

And setting out from there, they went again into Galilee, nor did he want anyone to know.

9:30 *docebat autem discipulos suos et dicebat illis quoniam Filius hominis tradetur in manus hominum et occident eum et occisus tertia die resurget*

But he taught his disciples, and said to them that, "Man's Son will be handed over into man's hands. And they will kill him and, *once* killed, he will rise *the* third day."

9:31 *at illi ignorabant verbum et timebant eum interrogare*

And they did not understand *the* word, and were afraid to ask him.

Power Over Ambition

9:32 *et venerunt Capharnaum qui cum domi esset interrogabat eos quid in via tractabatis*

And they came to Capernaum. *Jesus,*[25] when he was in *the* house, asked them, "What were you talking about on *the* road?"

9:33 *at illi tacebant siquidem inter se in via disputaverant quis esset illorum maior*

And they were silent, since they had been disputing among themselves on *the* way who of them was *the* greatest.

9:34 *et residens vocavit duodecim et ait illis si quis*

---

[25] Literally, "Who, when he was in the house . . ."

vult primus esse erit omnium novissimus et omnium minister

And, sitting down again, he called *the* twelve and said to them, "If someone wants to be first, he will be last of all, and minister of all."

9:35 *et accipiens puerum statuit eum in medio eorum quem cum conplexus esset ait illis*

And, receiving *a* boy, he stood him in their midst – whom, when he had hugged him, he said to them,

9:36 *quisquis unum ex huiusmodi pueris receperit in nomine meo me recipit et quicumque me susceperit non me suscipit sed eum qui me misit*

"Whoever receives one of such children in my name, receives me. And whoever supports me does not support me, but Him who sent me."

Power Over Sectarianism

9:37 *respondit illi Iohannes dicens magister vidimus quendam in nomine tuo eicientem daemonia qui non sequitur nos et prohibuimus eum*

John answered him, saying, "Teacher, we saw one who doesn't follow us throwing out demons in your name, and we stopped him.

9:38 *Iesus autem ait nolite prohibere eum nemo est enim qui faciat virtutem in nomine meo et possit cito male loqui de me*

But Jesus said, "Don't stop him – for *there* is no one who can work power in my name and quickly speak harm about me –

9:39 *qui enim non est adversum vos pro vobis est*

"for who is not against you is for you!

9:40 *quisquis enim potum dederit vobis calicem aquae in*

*nomine meo quia Christi estis
amen dico vobis non perdet
mercedem suam*

"For anyone who gives you *a*
cup of water in my name,
because you are of Christ –
Amen I say to you he will not
lose his reward.

Beware of What Separates
You from Christ

9:41 *et quisquis
scandalizaverit unum ex his
pusillis credentibus in me
bonum est ei magis si
circumdaretur mola asinaria
collo eius et in mare
mitteretur*

"And whoever scandalizes one
of these little ones believing in
me, it is better for him if *a*
millstone is draped around his
neck and he is thrown into *the*
sea.

9:42 *et si scandalizaverit te
manus tua abscide illam
bonum est tibi debilem introire
in vitam quam duas manus
habentem ire in gehennam in
ignem inextinguibilem*

"And if your hand scandalizes
you, cut it off! It is good for
you to enter into life disabled
than, having two hands, to go
to Gehenna, to
inextinguishable fire –

9:43 *ubi vermis eorum non
moritur et ignis non
extinguitur*

"where their worm does not
die, and fire is not put out.

9:44 *et si pes tuus te
scandalizat amputa illum
bonum est tibi claudum
introire in vitam aeternam
quam duos pedes habentem
mitti in gehennam ignis
inextinguibilis*

"And if your foot scandalizes
you, amputate it! It is better to
you to enter into eternal life
lame than, having two feet, to
be thrown into *the* Gehenna of
unquenchable fire –

9:45 *ubi vermis eorum non
moritur et ignis non
extinguitur*

"where their worm does not die, and fire is not put out.

9:46 *quod si oculus tuus scandalizat te eice eum bonum est tibi luscum introire in regnum Dei quam duos oculos habentem mitti in gehennam ignis*

"Yet if your eye scandalizes you, pluck it out! It is good for you to go one-eyed into God's kingdom than, having two eyes, to be thrown into *the* Gehenna of fire–

9:47 *ubi vermis eorum non moritur et ignis non extinguitur*

"where their worm does not die, and fire is not put out.

Every Victim
Will Be Salted
9:48 *omnis enim igne sallietur et omnis victima sallietur*

"For each *one* will be salted by fire, and every victim will be salted.[26]

9:49 *bonum est sal quod si sal insulsum fuerit in quo illud condietis habete in vobis sal et pacem habete inter vos*

"Salt is good, yet if salt becomes tasteless, in what can it be seasoned? Have salt in yourselves, and have peace among you!"

---

[26] See Leviticus 2:13.

Power to Interpret Ancient Law

Mark 10:1 *et inde exsurgens venit in fines Iudaeae ultra Iordanen et conveniunt iterum turbae ad eum et sicut consueverat iterum docebat illos*

And going out of there, he came to Judea's borders, beyond Jordan. And again *a* crowd comes together to him and, as was his custom, he again taught them.

10:2 *et accedentes Pharisaei interrogabant eum si licet viro uxorem dimittere temptantes eum*

And Pharisees, coming near, questioned him whether it was legal for *a* husband to divorce *a* wife, testing him.

10:3 *at ille respondens dixit eis quid vobis praecepit Moses*

And he, answering, said to them, "What did Moses command you?"

10:4 *qui dixerunt Moses permisit libellum repudii scribere et dimittere*

They[27] said, "Moses permitted *a man* to write *a* letter of repudiation, and to let *her* go."[28]

10:5 *quibus respondens Iesus ait ad duritiam cordis vestri scripsit vobis praeceptum istud*

Responding to them, Jesus said, "He wrote this commandment to you because of your hearts' hardness,

10:6 *ab initio autem creaturae masculum et feminam fecit eos Deus*

"but from *the* creature's beginning, God made them male and female.

10:7 *propter hoc relinquet*

---

[27] Literally, "Who said, 'Moses . . .'"

[28] See Deuteronomy 24:1-4.

*homo patrem suum et matrem
et adherebit ad uxorem suam*

"Because of this, *'A* man will leave his father and mother, and cling to his wife,

10:8 *et erunt duo in carne una itaque iam non sunt duo sed una caro*

"'and they will be two in one flesh'[29] – so that they are no longer two, but one flesh.

10:9 *quod ergo Deus iunxit homo non separet*

"What God joined, then, let man not separate."

The Disciples Struggle to Understand
10:10 *et in domo iterum discipuli eius de eodem interrogaverunt eum*

And again, in *the* house, some of his disciples asked him.

10:11 *et dicit illis quicumque*

---

[29] Genesis 2:24.

dimiserit uxorem suam et aliam duxerit adulterium committit super eam

And he says to them, "Whoever divorces his wife and marries another commits adultery against her.

10:12 *et si uxor dimiserit virum suum et alii nupserit moechatur*

"And if *a* wife divorces her husband and marries another, she commits adultery."

Power to Receive Offerings
10:13 *et offerebant illi parvulos ut tangeret illos discipuli autem comminabantur offerentibus*

And they offered him little children, so he could touch them. But *the* disciples threatened those offering *them.*

10:14 *quos cum videret Iesus indigne tulit et ait illis sinite parvulos venire ad me et ne prohibueritis eos talium est* *enim regnum Dei*

When Jesus had seen it, he took offense. And he said to them, "Let little ones come to me, and don't stop them – of such is God's kingdom!

10:15 *amen dico vobis quisque non receperit regnum Dei velut parvulus non intrabit in illud*

"Amen I say to you, whoever won't receive God's kingdom like *a* little one won't enter it."

10:16 *et conplexans eos et inponens manus super illos benedicebat eos*

And, embracing them and laying hands on them, he blessed them.

Power of Enduring Values
10:17 *et cum egressus esset in viam procurrens quidam genu flexo ante eum rogabat eum magister bone quid faciam ut vitam aeternam percipiam*

And when he had gone back out on *the* road, someone running up to him, bowing *the* knee before him, asked him, "Good master, what can I do so I can achieve eternal life?"

10:18 *Iesus autem dixit ei quid me dicis bonum nemo bonus nisi unus Deus*

But Jesus said to him, "Why do you call me good? No one *is* good except one – God.

10:19 *praecepta nosti ne adulteres ne occidas ne fureris ne falsum testimonium dixeris ne fraudem feceris honora patrem tuum et matrem*

"You've known *the* commandments:
You will not commit adultery.
You will not kill.
You will not steal.
You will not speak false testimony.
You will not work fraud.
Honor your father and mother."

10:20 *et ille respondens ait illi magister omnia haec conservavi a iuventute mea*

And he, answering, said to him, "Teacher, I've kept all these since my youth."

10:21 *Iesus autem intuitus eum dilexit eum et dixit illi unum tibi deest vade quaecumque habes vende et da pauperibus et habebis thesaurum in caelo et veni sequere me*

But Jesus, knowing him, delighted in him. And he said to him, "One *thing* is lacking to you. Go, sell whatever you have, and give to *the* poor – and you'll have treasure in *the* sky. And come follow me!"

10:22 *qui contristatus in verbo abiit maerens erat enim habens possessiones multas*

He,[30] saddened at *the* word, went out grieving, for he was

holding on to many possessions.

10:23 *et circumspiciens Iesus ait discipulis suis quam difficile qui pecunias habent in regnum Dei introibunt*

And looking around, Jesus said to his disciples, "How hard *it is* for *those* who hold on to money to go into God's kingdom!"

10:24 *discipuli autem obstupescebant in verbis eius at Iesus rursus respondens ait illis filioli quam difficile est confidentes in pecuniis regnum Dei introire*

But *the* disciples were astounded at his words. And Jesus, answering again, said to them, "Little children, how hard *it is* for those trusting in wealth to go into God's kingdom!

10:25 *facilius est camelum per foramen acus transire quam divitem intrare in regnum Dei*

---

[30] Literally, "Who, saddened at the word . . ."

"*It* is easier for *a* camel to go through *a* needle's eye, than *for a* rich man to go into God's kingdom.

10:26 *qui magis admirabantur dicentes ad semet ipsos et quis potest salvus fieri*

They were astounded all *the* more, saying to each other, "And who can be safe?"

10:27 *et intuens illos Iesus ait apud homines inpossibile est sed non apud Deum omnia enim possibilia sunt apud Deum*

And knowing them, Jesus said, "It's impossible with men, but not with God. All *of these* are possible with God.

10:28 *coepit Petrus ei dicere ecce nos dimisimus omnia et secuti sumus te*

Peter began to say to him, "Look, we've left all and followed you."

10:29 *respondens Iesus ait amen dico vobis nemo est qui reliquerit domum aut fratres aut sorores aut matrem aut patrem aut filios aut agros propter me et propter evangelium*

Jesus, answering, said, "Amen I say to you, *there* is no one who leaves house, or brothers, or sisters, or mother, or father, or children, or fields – for my sake, and for *the* good news –

10:30 *qui non accipiat centies tantum nunc in tempore hoc domos et fratres et sorores et matres et filios et agros cum persecutionibus et in saeculo futuro vitam aeternam*

"who may not receive *a* hundred times as much, not only now in this time – houses, and brothers, and sisters, and mothers, and children, and fields, with troubles[31] – and in *a* future age

---

[31] The Greek word is the genitive masculine plural of διωγμός, "pursuit, persecution,

eternal life.

10:31 *multi autem erunt primi novissimi et novissimi primi*

"But many first *ones* will be last, and last *ones* first.

Power to Face the Future
10:32 *erant autem in via ascendentes in Hierosolyma et praecedebat illos Iesus et stupebant et sequentes timebant et adsumens iterum duodecim coepit illis dicere quae essent ei ventura*

But they were going up to Jerusalem on *the* road, and Jesus went before them. And they were astounded and fearful, following *him*. And, again taking up *the* twelve, he began to say to them what was to happen to him –

10:33 *quia ecce ascendimus in Hierosolyma et Filius hominis tradetur principibus sacerdotum et scribis et senioribus et damnabunt eum*

_____

harassment."

morti et tradent eum gentibus

that, "Look, we'll go up to Jerusalem. And man's Son will be handed over to *the* priests' princes, and writers, and elders. And they will damn him to death, and hand him over to *the* nations.

10:34 *et inludent ei et conspuent eum et flagellabunt eum et interficient eum et tertia die resurget*

"And they will mock him, and spit on him, and beat him, and kill him. And *the* third day he will rise again."

Jacob and John
Ask for Privilege
10:35 *et accedunt ad illum Iacobus et Iohannes filii Zebedaei dicentes magister volumus ut quodcumque petierimus facias nobis*

And Jacob and John, Zebedee's sons, come to him, saying, "Teacher, we want that whatever we ask, you'll do *it* for us."

10:36 *at ille dixit eis quid vultis ut faciam vobis*

And he said to them, "What do you want that I can do for you?"

10:37 *et dixerunt da nobis ut unus ad dexteram tuam et alius ad sinistram tuam sedeamus in gloria tua*

And they said to him, "Give to us that we can sit, one at your right and *the* other at your left – in your glory."

10:38 *Iesus autem ait eis nescitis quid petatis potestis bibere calicem quem ego bibo aut baptismum quo ego baptizor baptizari*

But Jesus said to them, "You don't know what you're asking. Can you drink *the* cup that I'm drinking, or be baptized in *the* baptism I'm baptized in?

10:39 *at illi dixerunt ei possumus Iesus autem ait eis calicem quidem quem ego*

bibo bibetis et baptismum quo ego baptizor baptizabimini

And they said to him, "We can."

But Jesus said to them, "You'll indeed drink *the* cup that I'm drinking, and you'll be baptized in *the* baptism I'm baptized in.

10:40 *sedere autem ad dexteram meam vel ad sinistram non est meum dare sed quibus paratum est*

"But to sit at my right or at *my* left isn't mine to give – yet to *those* for whom it's readied."

Power to Refocus Indignation

10:41 *et audientes decem coeperunt indignari de Iacobo et Iohanne*

And hearing *this*, *the* ten began to be indignant at Jacob and John.

10:42 *Iesus autem vocans eos ait illis scitis quia hii qui* *videntur principari gentibus dominantur eis et principes eorum potestatem habent ipsorum*

But Jesus, calling them, said to them, "You know that those who seem to be princes among nations dominate them, and their princes have power over them.

10:43 *non ita est autem in vobis sed quicumque voluerit fieri maior erit vester minister*

"It isn't like that with you, but whoever wants to be great will be your minister.

10:44 *et quicumque voluerit in vobis primus esse erit omnium servus*

And whoever wants to be first among you will be slave of all.

10:45 *nam et Filius hominis non venit ut ministraretur ei sed ut ministraret et daret animam suam redemptionem pro multis*

"For man's Son also did not come so he could be ministered to, yet so he could minister – and give his soul as *a* buying back of many."

Power to Give Vision

10:46 *et veniunt Hierichum et proficiscente eo de Hiericho et discipulis eius et plurima multitudine filius Timei Bartimeus caecus sedebat iuxta viam mendicans*

And they come to Jericho. And he *was* setting out from there with both *the* disciples and *a* large crowd. And Timeus's son, Bar-timeus, *a* blind *man*, sat begging alongside *the* road –

10:47 *qui cum audisset quia Iesus Nazarenus est coepit clamare et dicere Fili David Iesu miserere mei*

who, when he'd heard that it was Jesus Nazarene, began to shout and say, "David's Son, Jesus, have mercy on me!"

10:48 *et comminabantur illi*

multi ut taceret at ille multo
magis clamabat Fili David
miserere mei

And they threatened him much that he shut up. And he shouted even more, "David's Son, have mercy on me!"

10:49 *et stans Iesus praecepit illum vocari et vocant caecum dicentes ei animaequior esto surge vocat te*

And Jesus, stopping, commanded him to be called. And they call *the* blind man, saying to him, "Calm down! Get up! He's calling you."

10:50 *qui proiecto vestimento suo exiliens venit ad eum*

The blind man,[32] throwing off his coat, jumping up, came to him.

10:51 *et respondens illi Iesus dixit quid vis tibi faciam caecus autem dixit ei rabboni*

ut videam

And answering him, Jesus said, "What do you want that I can do for you?"

But *the* blind man said to him, "Rabbi, that I can see!"

10:52 *Iesus autem ait illi vade fides tua te salvum fecit et confestim vidit et sequebatur eum in via*

But Jesus said to him, "Go! Your faith has made you well."

And at once he sees, and follows him on *the* road.

---

[32] Literally, "Who, throwing off his coat . . ."

Jesus Prepares
to Enter Jerusalem

Mark 11:1 *et cum adpropinquarent Hierosolymae et Bethaniae ad montem Olivarum mittit duos ex discipulis suis*

And when they had come near Jerusalem and Bethany, to *the* Mount of Olives, he sends two of his disciples.

11:2 *et ait illis ite in castellum quod est contra vos et statim introeuntes illuc invenietis pullum ligatum super quem nemo adhuc hominum sedit solvite illum et adducite*

And he said to them, "Go into *the* town that is across, and, as soon as you enter it, you'll find *a* colt tied up, which no one has sat on yet. Untie him, and bring him.

11:3 *et si quis vobis dixerit quid facitis dicite quia Domino necessarius est et continuo illum dimittet huc*

"And if someone asks you, 'What are you doing?' – say that, "*It* is necessary to *the* Lord, and he will send him here at once."

11:4 *et abeuntes invenerunt pullum ligatum ante ianuam foris in bivio et solvunt eum*

And going out, they found *the* colt tied before *a* door, outside at *a* crossroad, and they untie him.

11:5 *et quidam de illic stantibus dicebant illis quid facitis solventes pullum*

And some of those standing there said to them, "What are you doing untying *the* colt?"

11:6 *qui dixerunt eis sicut praeceperat illis Iesus et dimiserunt eis*

They[33] spoke to them as Jesus had commanded them, and *the others* let *the colt* go with

---

[33] Literally, "Who spoke to them . . ."

them.

11:7 *et duxerunt pullum ad Iesum et inponunt illi vestimenta sua et sedit super eo*

And they led *the* colt to Jesus, and put their coats on him, and he sat on him.

Jesus Enters Jerusalem
11:8 *multi autem vestimenta sua straverunt in via alii autem frondes caedebant de arboribus et sternebant in via*

But many lay their coats on *the* road, and others cut branches from *the* trees and placed them on *the* road.

11:9 *et qui praeibant et qui sequebantur clamabant dicentes osanna benedictus qui venit in nomine Domini*

And those who went before and those who followed shouted, saying, "Hosanna! Blessed *is he* who comes in

the Lord's name![34]

11:10 *benedictum quod venit regnum patris nostri David osanna in excelsis*

"Blessed is *the* kingdom of our father David, which is coming! Hosanna in *the* highest!"

11:11 *et introivit Hierosolyma in templum et circumspectis omnibus cum iam vespera esset hora exivit in Bethania cum duodecim*

And he went into Jerusalem, to *the* temple. And looking around at all, when it was already *the* hour of evening, he went out to Bethany with *the* twelve.

Power to Curse the Unfruitful
11:12 *et alia die cum exirent a Bethania esuriit*

And *the* next day when he left from Bethany, he was hungry.

---

[34] See Psalm 118:26.

11:13 *cumque vidisset a longe ficum habentem folia venit si quid forte inveniret in ea et cum venisset ad eam nihil invenit praeter folia non enim erat tempus ficorum*

And when he had seen from far off *a* fig tree having leaves, he comes to see if perhaps he can find something on it. And when he had come to it, he found nothing except leaves, for it wasn't *the* season for figs.

11:14 *et respondens dixit ei iam non amplius in aeternum quisquam fructum ex te manducet et audiebant discipuli eius*

And responding, he said to it, "Let no one eat fruit from you any more in eternity."

And his disciples heard *this*.

11:15 *et veniunt Hierosolymam et cum introisset templum coepit eicere vendentes et ementes in templo et mensas*

nummulariorum et cathedras vendentium columbas evertit

And they come to Jerusalem, and when he had gone into *the* temple, he began to throw out *the* sellers and buyers in *the* temple. And he overturned *the* money changers' tables, and *the* seats of those selling doves.

11:16 *et non sinebat ut quisquam vas transferret per templum*

And he didn't permit that anyone could carry *a* vessel through *the* temple.

11:17 *et docebat dicens eis non scriptum est quia domus mea domus orationis vocabitur omnibus gentibus vos autem fecistis eam speluncam latronum*

And he taught, saying to them, "Isn't it written that 'My house will be called *a* house of prayer for all nations?'[35] Yet

---

[35] Isaiah 56:7.

you've made her 'a cave for thieves.'"[36]

11:18 *quo audito principes sacerdotum et scribae quaerebant quomodo eum perderent timebant enim eum quoniam universa turba admirabatur super doctrina eius*

Hearing this, *the* priests' princes and *the* writers sought how they could kill him, for they were afraid of him – because *the* whole crowd admired his teaching.

11:19 *et cum vespera facta esset egrediebatur de civitate*

And when evening came, he went out of *the* city.

11:20 *et cum mane transirent viderunt ficum aridam factam a radicibus*

And when they passed through early, they saw *the* fig tree made dry from *the* roots.

---

[36] Jeremiah 7:11.

11:21 *et recordatus Petrus dicit ei rabbi ecce ficus cui maledixisti aruit*

And Peter, remembering, says to him, "Rabbi, look! *The* fig tree that you cursed dried up."

Power of Certain Prayer
11:22 *et respondens Iesus ait illis habete fidem Dei*

And Jesus, answering, said to them, "Have God's faith!

11:23 *amen dico vobis quicumque dixerit huic monti tollere et mittere in mare et non haesitaverit in corde suo sed crediderit quia quodcumque dixerit fiat fiet ei*

"Amen I say to you, whoever says to this mountain, 'Be taken up and thrown into *the* sea,' and doesn't hesitate in his heart, but believes that whatever he said can be done – it will be done for him!

11:24 *propterea dico vobis omnia quaecumque orantes petitis credite quia accipietis* *et veniet vobis*

"For this reason I'm saying to you, believe that you will receive all – whatever you ask, praying – and they will come to you!

11:25 *et cum stabitis ad orandum dimittite si quid habetis adversus aliquem ut et Pater vester qui in caelis est dimittat vobis peccata vestra*

"And when you will stand to pray, forgive, if you have something against anyone, so your Father also, who is in *the* skies, may forgive your sins for you!

11:26 *quod si vos non dimiseritis nec Pater vester qui in caelis est dimittet vobis peccata vestra*

"Yet if you won't forgive, neither will your Father who is in *the* skies forgive your sins for you."

Power Over Impertinent Questions

11:27 *et veniunt rursus Hierosolymam et cum ambularet in templo accedunt ad eum summi sacerdotes et scribae et seniores*

And they come again to Jerusalem and, while he walked in *the* temple, *the* high priests and writers and elders come to him.

11:28 *et dicunt illi in qua potestate haec facis et quis tibi dedit hanc potestatem ut ista facias*

And they say to him, "By what authority are you doing these *things*, and who gave you this authority so you do them?"

11:29 *Iesus autem respondens ait illis interrogabo vos et ego unum verbum et respondete mihi et dicam vobis in qua potestate haec faciam*

But Jesus, answering, said to them, "I will question you, too, one word, and you respond to me! And I'll say to you by what authority I'm doing these.

11:30 *baptismum Iohannis de caelo erat an ex hominibus respondete mihi*

"Was John's baptism from heaven or from men? Answer me!"

11:31 *at illi cogitabant secum dicentes si dixerimus de caelo dicet quare ergo non credidistis ei*

And they thought to themselves, saying, "If we say, 'From heaven,' he'll say, 'Why didn't you believe him, then?'

11:32 *sed dicemus ex hominibus timebant populum omnes enim habebant Iohannem quia vere propheta esset*

"Yet can we say from men?"

They were afraid of *the* people, for all held that John was truly *a* prophet.

11:33 *et respondentes dicunt Iesu nescimus respondens Iesus ait illis neque ego dico vobis in qua potestate haec faciam*

And answering, they say to Jesus, "We don't know."

Jesus, answering, said to them, "Neither do I tell you by what authority I do these."

Power to Announce Judgment for Sin

Mark 12:1 *et coepit illis in parabolis loqui vineam pastinavit homo et circumdedit sepem et fodit lacum et aedificavit turrem et locavit eam agricolis et peregre profectus est*

And he began to talk to them in comparisons. "*A* man prepared *a* vineyard, and made *a* hedge around it, and dug *a* pit, and built *a* tower. And he placed workers in it, and set out to go abroad.

12:2 *et misit ad agricolas in tempore servum ut ab agricolis acciperet de fructu vineae*

"And he sent *a* slave to *the* workers at *the* season, so he could receive some of *the* vineyard's fruit from *the* workers –

12:3 *qui adprehensum eum ceciderunt et dimiserunt vacuum*

"who, seizing him, struck *him* and sent *him* away empty.

12:4 *et iterum misit ad illos alium servum et illum capite vulneraverunt et contumeliis adfecerunt*

"And again, he sent another slave to them, and him they wounded in *the* head and harmed by abuses.

12:5 *et rursum alium misit et illum occiderunt et plures alios quosdam caedentes alios vero occidentes*

"And again he sent another, and him they killed – and many others, some of whom they beat, and others they killed.

12:6 *adhuc ergo unum habens filium carissimum et illum misit ad eos novissimum dicens quia reverebuntur filium meum*

"Therefore, still having one, *a* most beloved son, he sent him also to them at *the* end, saying that, 'They will reverence my son.'

12:7 *coloni autem dixerunt ad invicem hic est heres venite occidamus eum et nostra erit hereditas*

"But *the* tenants said to themselves, 'This is *the* heir. Come, let's kill him, and *the* inheritance will be ours!'

12:8 *et adprehendentes eum occiderunt et eiecerunt extra vineam*

"And seizing him, they killed *him* and threw *him* out of *the* vineyard.

12:9 *quid ergo faciet dominus vineae veniet et perdet colonos et dabit vineam aliis*

"What, then, will *the* vineyard's lord do? He will come and destroy *the* tenants, and give *the* vineyard to others.

12:10 *nec scripturam hanc legistis lapidem quem*

reprobaverunt aedificantes hic factus est in caput anguli

"Haven't you read this scripture? '*The* stone that *the* builders rejected, this has been made into *the* corner's head.

12:11 *a Domino factum est istud et est mirabile in oculis nostris*

"'This came from *the* Lord, and it is wonderful in our eyes.'"[37]

12:12 *et quaerebant eum tenere et timuerunt turbam cognoverunt enim quoniam ad eos parabolam hanc dixerit et relicto eo abierunt*

And they wanted to seize him, yet they feared *the* crowd, for they recognized that he spoke this comparison about them. And leaving him, they went out.

---

[37] Psalm 118:22-23.

Power to Maintain Perspective

12:13 *et mittunt ad eum quosdam ex Pharisaeis et Herodianis ut eum caperent in verbo*

And they send some of *the* Pharisees and Herodians to him so they could capture him in word –

12:14 *qui venientes dicunt ei magister scimus quoniam verax es et non curas quemquam nec enim vides in faciem hominis sed in veritate viam Dei doces licet dari tributum Caesari an non dabimus*

who, coming, say to him, "Teacher, we know that you are true, and you don't favor anyone – for you don't look on *a* man's face, but you teach God's way in truth. Is it lawful to give tribute to Caesar, or will we not give?"

12:15 *qui sciens versutiam eorum ait illis quid me temptatis adferte mihi*

denarium ut videam

Jesus,[38] knowing their deceit, said to them, "Why are you testing me? Bring me *a* denarius so I can see it."

12:16 *at illi adtulerunt et ait illis cuius est imago haec et inscriptio dicunt illi Caesaris*

And they brought it, and he said to them, "Whose image and inscription is this?"

They say to him, "Caesar's."

12:17 *respondens autem Iesus dixit illis reddite igitur quae sunt Caesaris Caesari et quae sunt Dei Deo et mirabantur super eo*

But Jesus, answering, said to them, "Then, give what are Caesar's to Caesar, and what are God's to God."

And they were amazed at him.

---

[38] Literally, "Who, knowing their deceit . . ."

Questioned about
the Resurrection

12:18 *et venerunt ad eum Sadducaei qui dicunt resurrectionem non esse et interrogabant eum dicentes*

And Sadducees came to him, who say there is no resurrection. And they asked him, saying,

12:19 *magister Moses nobis scripsit ut si cuius frater mortuus fuerit et dimiserit uxorem et filios non reliquerit accipiat frater eius uxorem ipsius et resuscitet semen fratri suo*

"Teacher, Moses wrote us that if *a* brother should die and leave *a* wife, yet not leave sons, his brother should receive his wife and raise up seed to his brother.[39]

12:20 *septem ergo fratres erant et primus accepit uxorem et mortuus est non*

---

[39] See Deuteronomy 25:5-10.

relicto semine

"So there were seven brothers, and *the* first received *a* wife and died, not leaving seed.

12:21 *et secundus accepit eam et mortuus est et nec iste reliquit semen et tertius similiter*

"And *the* second received her and died, and neither did he leave seed, and *the* third likewise.

12:22 *et acceperunt eam similiter septem et non reliquerunt semen novissima omnium defuncta est et mulier*

"And *the* seven likewise received her, and didn't leave seed. Last of all, *the* woman also died.

12:23 *in resurrectione ergo cum resurrexerint cuius de his erit uxor septem enim habuerunt eam uxorem*

"In *the* resurrection, therefore, when they are raised, whose wife will she be – for seven had her *as* wife?"

12:24 *et respondens Iesus ait illis non ideo erratis non scientes scripturas neque virtutem Dei*

And Jesus, answering, said to them, "Isn't this why you are wrong, knowing neither scriptures nor God's power?

12:25 *cum enim a mortuis resurrexerint neque nubent neque nubentur sed sunt sicut angeli in caelis*

"For when they are raised from *the* dead, they neither marry nor are married, but are like angels in *the* sky.

12:26 *de mortuis autem quod resurgant non legistis in libro Mosi super rubum quomodo dixerit illi Deus inquiens ego sum Deus Abraham et Deus Isaac et Deus Iacob*

"But that they rise from *the* dead, haven't you read in Moses' book, about *the* bush,

how God spoke to him saying, 'I am Abraham's God, and Isaac's God, and Jacob's God'?[40]

12:27 *non est Deus mortuorum sed vivorum vos ergo multum erratis*

"He is not God of *the* dead but of *the* living. You therefore err greatly."

Which Commandment Is First?

12:28 *et accessit unus de scribis qui audierat illos conquirentes et videns quoniam bene illis responderit interrogavit eum quod esset primum omnium mandatum*

And one of *the* writers came, who heard them questioning him. And seeing that he answered them well, he asked him, "What was *the* first commandment of all?"

12:29 *Iesus autem respondit ei quia primum omnium*

---

[40] Exodus 3:6.

mandatum est audi Israhel Dominus Deus noster Deus unus est

But Jesus answered him that, "*The* first commandment of all is, 'Hear, Israel, *the* Lord our God is one God.'*[41]*

12:30 *et diliges Dominum Deum tuum ex toto corde tuo et ex tota anima tua et ex tota mente tua et ex tota virtute tua hoc est primum mandatum*

"'And you will delight in *the* Lord your God from all your heart, and from all your soul, and from all your mind, and from all your strength.' This is *the* first commandment.

12:31 *secundum autem simile illi diliges proximum tuum tamquam te ipsum maius horum aliud mandatum non est*

"But *the* second is like it: 'You will delight in your neighbor as yourself.' No other

[41] Deuteronomy 6:4.

commandment is greater than these."

12:32 *et ait illi scriba bene magister in veritate dixisti quia unus est et non est alius praeter eum*

And *the* writer said to him, "Well, teacher! You've said in truth that He is one, and *there* is no other before Him,

12:33 *et ut diligatur ex toto corde et ex toto intellectu et ex tota anima et ex tota fortitudine et diligere proximum tamquam se ipsum maius est omnibus holocaustomatibus et sacrificiis*

"and that to delight from all *the* heart, and from all *the* intellect, and from all *the* soul, and from all *the* strength, and to delight in neighbor as oneself – this is greater than all burnt offerings and sacrifices."

12:34 *Iesus autem videns quod sapienter respondisset*

dixit illi non es longe a regno Dei et nemo iam audebat eum interrogare

But Jesus, seeing that he had answered wisely, said to him, "You aren't far from God's kingdom."

And thereafter no one dared to question him.

Whose Son Is Christ?

12:35 *et respondens Iesus dicebat docens in templo quomodo dicunt scribae Christum Filium esse David*

And Jesus, answering, spoke *while* teaching in *the* temple, "How do *the* writers say Christ is David's Son?

12:36 *ipse enim David dicit in Spiritu Sancto dixit Dominus Domino meo sede a dextris meis donec ponam inimicos tuos scabillum pedum tuorum*

"For David himself says in *the* Holy Spirit, '*The* Lord said to my Lord, Sit at my right hand, until I place your enemies *as* your footstool.'

12:37 *ipse ergo David dicit eum Dominum et unde est filius eius et multa turba eum libenter audivit*

"So David himself calls him 'Lord.' And how is he his son?"

And the great crowd heard him freely.

Beware of Pride of Position

12:38 *et dicebat eis in doctrina sua cavete a scribis qui volunt in stolis ambulare et salutari in foro*

And he said to them in his teaching, "Beware of *the* writers, who want to walk around in formal dress, and be saluted in *the* street,

12:39 *et in primis cathedris sedere in synagogis et primos discubitus in cenis*

"and to sit in *the* first seats in *the* synagogues, and *the* first places at dinners –

12:40 *qui devorant domos viduarum sub obtentu prolixae orationis hii accipient prolixius iudicium*

"who devour widows' houses under *the* pretext of wordy prayers. These will receive wordy judgment."

Power to Discern a Genuine Gift

12:41 *et sedens Iesus contra gazofilacium aspiciebat quomodo turba iactaret aes in gazofilacium et multi divites iactabant multa*

And Jesus, sitting across from *the* treasury, watched how *the* crowd threw coins into *the* treasury. And many rich *people* put in much.

12:42 *cum venisset autem una vidua pauper misit duo minuta quod est quadrans*

But when *a* poor widow had come, she threw *in* two small coins – that is, *a* quarter.

12:43 *et convocans discipulos suos ait illis amen dico vobis quoniam vidua haec pauper plus omnibus misit qui miserunt in gazofilacium*

And calling together his disciples, he said to them, "Amen I say to you that this poor widow put in more than all those who put into *the* treasury.

12:44 *omnes enim ex eo quod abundabat illis miserunt haec vero de penuria sua omnia quae habuit misit totum victum suum*

"For all of them put in out of what was abundant to them, but she from her poverty put in all that she had – all her living."

Power to Foretell
the Future

Mark 13:1 *et cum egrederetur de templo ait illi unus ex discipulis suis magister aspice quales lapides et quales structurae*

And when they went out from *the* temple, one of his disciples said to him, 'Teacher, see what stones and what structures!"

13:2 *et respondens Iesus ait illi vides has omnes magnas aedificationes non relinquetur lapis super lapidem qui non destruatur*

And Jesus, answering, said to him, "You see all these great buildings? Not one stone will be left on another which won't be destroyed."

13:3 *et cum sederet in montem Olivarum contra templum interrogabant eum separatim Petrus et Iacobus et Iohannes et Andreas*

And when he sat on *the* Mount of Olives across from *the* temple, Peter, and Jacob, and John, and Andrew asked him separately,

13:4 *dic nobis quando ista fient et quod signum erit quando haec omnia incipient consummari*

"Tell us when these things will happen, and what sign will be when all these begin to take place?"

Signs of the End of the Age

13:5 *et respondens Iesus coepit dicere illis videte ne quis vos seducat*

And Jesus, answering, began to say to them, "Watch out, unless someone seduce you!

13:6 *multi enim venient in nomine meo dicentes quia ego sum et multos seducent*

"For many will come in my name, saying that, 'I am,' and they will seduce many.

13:7 *cum audieritis autem*

bella et opiniones bellorum ne timueritis oportet enim fieri sed nondum finis

"But when you hear of wars and rumors of wars, don't be afraid – for it must be, yet *the* end *is* not yet.

13:8 *exsurget autem gens super gentem et regnum super regnum et erunt terraemotus per loca et fames initium dolorum haec*

"But nation will rise against nation, and kingdom against kingdom, and earthquakes and famines will be in *various* places. These are *the* sorrows' beginning.

13:9 *videte autem vosmet ipsos tradent enim vos conciliis et in synagogis vapulabitis et ante praesides et reges stabitis propter me in testimonium illis*

"Yet see to yourselves, for they will hand you over to councils, and you will be beaten in synagogues. And you will stand before governors and kings for my sake, in testimony to them.

13:10 *et in omnes gentes primum oportet praedicari evangelium*

"And *the* good news must first be preached among all nations.

13:11 *et cum duxerint vos tradentes nolite praecogitare quid loquamini sed quod datum vobis fuerit in illa hora id loquimini non enim estis vos loquentes sed Spiritus Sanctus*

"And when they lead you to hand *you* over, don't plan in advance what you will say. Yet what will be given to you in that hour, speak that – for you will not be speaking, but *the* Holy Spirit!

13:12 *tradet autem frater fratrem in mortem et pater filium et consurgent filii in parentes et morte adficient eos*

"But brother will hand over

brother to death, and father *a* son. And children will rise up against parents and cause them death.

13:13 *et eritis odio omnibus propter nomen meum qui autem sustinuerit in finem hic salvus erit*

"And you will be hated by all because of my name, yet who sustains to *the* end, he will be secured.

A Desolating Abomination
13:14 *cum autem videritis abominationem desolationis stantem ubi non debet qui legit intellegat tunc qui in Iudaea sunt fugiant in montes*

"But when you see *a* desolating abomination standing where it ought not – let who reads understand! – then, let *those* who are in Judea flee to *the* mountains.

13:15 *et qui super tectum ne descendat in domum nec introeat ut tollat quid de domo sua*

"And let one who is on *the* roof not come down into *the* house, nor enter *it* so he can take something from his house.

13:16 *et qui in agro erit non revertatur retro tollere vestimentum suum*

"And let no one who will be in *the* field turn back to take his clothing.

13:17 *vae autem praegnatibus et nutrientibus in illis diebus*

"Yet woe to those pregnant and nursing in those days!

13:18 *orate vero ut hieme non fiant*

"Pray, indeed, that they not come in winter,

13:19 *erunt enim dies illi tribulationes tales quales non fuerunt ab initio creaturae quam condidit Deus usque nunc neque fient* "for those days will be tribulations, *the* likes of which have not been since *the* creature's beginning which God established, even to now – nor will they come.

13:20 *et nisi breviasset Dominus dies non fuisset salva omnis caro sed propter electos quos elegit breviavit dies*

"And had *the* Lord not shortened *the* days, no flesh would have been secured. Yet for *the* chosen *ones*' sake, He shortened *the* days.

Beware of False Christs!
13:21 *et tunc si quis vobis dixerit ecce hic est Christus ecce illic ne credideritis*

"And then, if someone says to you, 'Look, Christ is here! Look, there!' – don't believe *it*!

13:22 *exsurgent enim p s e u d o c h r i s t i e t pseudoprophetae et dabunt signa et portenta ad seducendos si potest fieri*

etiam electos

"For false Christs and false prophets will rise up, and will give signs and wonders to seducing even *the* chosen ones – if it can be done.

13:23 *vos ergo videte ecce praedixi vobis omnia*

"Therefore you keep watch! Look, I've told you all beforehand.

Signs of a Disintegrating World Order
13:24 *sed in illis diebus post tribulationem illam sol contenebrabitur et luna non dabit splendorem suum*

"Yet in those days, after that trouble, *the* sun will be shadowed over and *the* moon will not give its splendor.

13:25 *et erunt stellae caeli decidentes et virtutes quae sunt in caelis movebuntur*

"And *the* sky's stars will be falling, and *the* powers that are in *the* sky will be moved.

13:26 *et tunc videbunt Filium hominis venientem in nubibus cum virtute multa et gloria*

"And then they will see man's Son coming in *the* clouds, with much power and glory.

13:27 *et tunc mittet angelos suos et congregabit electos suos a quattuor ventis a summo terrae usque ad summum caeli*

"And then he will send his angels, and he will gather his chosen *ones* together from *the* four winds, from earth's summit even to *the* sky's summit.

Signs to Look For

13:28 *a ficu autem discite parabolam cum iam ramus eius tener fuerit et nata fuerint folia cognoscitis quia in proximo sit aestas*

"Yet learn this comparison from *the* fig tree. When its branches are already tender,

and *the* leaves are brought forth, you know that summer is near

13:29 *sic et vos cum videritis haec fieri scitote quod in proximo sit in ostiis*

"So also you, when you see these happening, know that it is near, at *the* gates.

13:30 *amen dico vobis quoniam non transiet generatio haec donec omnia ista fiant*

"Amen I say to you that this generation will not pass away until all these happen.

13:31 *caelum et terra transibunt verba autem mea non transibunt*

"Sky and land will pass away, but my words will not pass away.

13:32 *de die autem illo vel hora nemo scit neque angeli in caelo neque Filius nisi Pater*

"Yet of that day or hour no one knows: neither angels in heaven, nor *the* Son – only *the* Father.

13:33 *videte vigilate et orate nescitis enim quando tempus sit*

"Look out! Keep watch and pray, for you don't know when *the* time may be.

13:34 *sicut homo qui peregre profectus reliquit domum suam et dedit servis suis potestatem cuiusque operis et ianitori praecipiat ut vigilet*

As *a* man who, setting out abroad, left his house and gave his slaves power over *the* works, and commands *the* doorkeeper that he keep watch –

13:35 *vigilate ergo nescitis enim quando dominus domus veniat sero an media nocte an galli cantu an mane*

"therefore, keep watch, for you don't know when *the*

house's master may come – at evening, or midnight, or cock-crow, or morning –

13:36 *ne cum venerit repente inveniat vos dormientes*

"unless, when he comes suddenly, he find you sleeping!

13:37 *quod autem vobis dico omnibus dico vigilate*

"But what I say to you, I say to all – keep watch!"

The Plot to Seize Jesus
Mark 14:1 *erat autem pascha et azyma post biduum et quaerebant summi sacerdotes et scribae quomodo eum dolo tenerent et occiderent*

But after two days it was Passover and unleavened bread, and *the* high priests and *the* writers sought how they could seize him by deceit and kill *him*,

14:2 *dicebant enim non in die festo ne forte tumultus fieret populi*

for they said, "Not on a feast day, unless *a* riot happen among *the* people."

Jesus Anointed for Burial
14:3 *et cum esset Bethaniae in domo Simonis leprosi et recumberet venit mulier habens alabastrum unguenti nardi spicati pretiosi et fracto alabastro effudit super caput eius*

And when he was at Bethany in *the* house of Simon *the* leper and reclining *at table, a* woman came to him, having *an* alabaster jar of costly spikenard ointment. And, breaking *the* alabaster, she poured *the ointment* over his head.

14:4 *erant autem quidam indigne ferentes intra semet ipsos et dicentes ut quid perditio ista unguenti facta est*

But some spoke indignantly among themselves, and saying that, "Why has this waste of ointment happened,

14:5 *poterat enim unguentum istud veniri plus quam trecentis denariis et dari pauperibus et fremebant in eam*

"for this ointment could have sold for more than three hundred days' wages, and been given to *the* poor?"

And they raged at her.

14:6 *Iesus autem dixit sinite eam quid illi molesti estis* *bonum opus operata est in me*

But Jesus said, "Leave her alone! Why are you bothering her? She's done *a* good work to me –

14:7 *semper enim pauperes habetis vobiscum et cum volueritis potestis illis benefacere me autem non semper habetis*

"for you'll always have *the* poor with you, and you can do well for them whenever you want. But you won't always have me.

14:8 *quod habuit haec fecit praevenit unguere corpus meum in sepulturam*

"What she had, she did. She comes before to anoint my body for burial.

14:9 *amen dico vobis ubicumque praedicatum fuerit evangelium istud in universum mundum et quod fecit haec narrabitur in memoriam eius*

"Amen I say to you, wherever this good news is preached in all *the* world, what she has done also will be told – in her memory."

Judas Seeks to Betray Jesus
14:10 *et Iudas Scariotis unus de duodecim abiit ad summos sacerdotes ut proderet eum illis*

And Judas Scarioth, one of *the* twelve, went out to *the* high priests, so he could betray him to them.

14:11 *qui audientes gavisi sunt et promiserunt ei pecuniam se daturos et quaerebat quomodo illum oportune traderet*

They,[42] hearing, were happy, and they promised him he would be given money. And he sought how he could hand him over conveniently.

---

[42] Literally, "Who, hearing . . ."

Preparation for
the Passover

14:12 *et primo die azymorum quando pascha immolabant dicunt ei discipuli quo vis eamus et paremus tibi ut manduces pascha*

And on *the* first day of unleavened bread, when *the* Passover lambs were offered, *the* disciples say to him, "Where do you want that we go and prepare for you, so you can eat *the* Passover?"

14:13 *et mittit duos ex discipulis suis et dicit eis ite in civitatem et occurret vobis homo laguenam aquae baiulans sequimini eum*

And he sends two of his disciples, and he says to them, "Go into *the* city, and *a* man carrying *a* bottle of water will meet you. Follow him,

14:14 *et quocumque introierit dicite domino domus quia magister dicit ubi est refectio mea ubi pascha cum discipulis meis manducem*

"and wherever he enters, say to *the* house's lord that, '*The* teacher says, Where is my dining room, where I can eat *the* Passover with my disciples?'

14:15 *et ipse vobis demonstrabit cenaculum grande stratum et illic parate nobis*

"And he will show you *a* large upper room, spread out. Prepare for us there."

14:16 *et abierunt discipuli eius et venerunt in civitatem et invenerunt sicut dixerat illis et praeparaverunt pascha*

And his disciples went out and came into *the* city. And they found *things* as he said to them, and they prepared *the* Passover.

Power to See

14:17 *vespere autem facto venit cum duodecim*

But when evening had come, he came with *the* twelve.

14:18 *et discumbentibus eis et manducantibus ait Iesus amen dico vobis quia unus ex vobis me tradet qui manducat mecum*

And reclining *at table* with them and eating, Jesus said, "Amen I say to you that one of you will hand me over – *one* who is eating with me.

14:19 *at illi coeperunt contristari et dicere ei singillatim numquid ego*

And they began to be sad together, and to say to him – each one – "It *isn't* me, is it?"

14:20 *qui ait illis unus ex duodecim qui intinguit mecum in catino*

Jesus[43] said to them, "One of *the* twelve who dips *bread* in *the* plate with me.

14:21 *et Filius quidem hominis vadit sicut scriptum*

---

[43] Literally, "Who said to them . . ."

est de eo vae autem homini illi per quem Filius hominis traditur bonum ei si non esset natus homo ille

"And man's Son indeed goes as is written about him, but woe to *the* man through whom man's Son is handed over – better for him if that man had not been born!"

This Is My Body
14:22 *et manducantibus illis accepit Iesus panem et benedicens fregit et dedit eis et ait sumite hoc est corpus meum*

And while they were eating, Jesus took bread.   And, blessing, he broke *it* and gave *it* to them.   And he said, "Take. This is my body."

This Is My Blood
14:23 *et accepto calice gratias agens dedit eis et biberunt ex illo omnes*

And taking *a* cup, giving thanks, he gave *it* to them. And all of them drank from it.

14:24 *et ait illis hic est sanguis meus novi testamenti qui pro multis effunditur*

And he said to them, "This is my blood of *the* new testament, who[44] is poured out for many.

14:25 *amen dico vobis quod iam non bibam de genimine vitis usque in diem illum cum illud bibam novum in regno Dei*

"Amen I say to you that I will not drink again from *the* fruit of *the* vine until that day when I drink it new in God's kingdom."

Power to Bear Denial
14:26 *et hymno dicto exierunt in montem Olivarum*

And *having* sung *a* hymn, they went out to *the* Mount of Olives.

---

[44] Note that blood is not impersonal here. Blood is personal, denoted by a "who," rather than a "what."

14:27 *et ait eis Iesus omnes scandalizabimini in nocte ista quia scriptum est percutiam pastorem et dispergentur oves*

And Jesus said to them, "All *of you* will be scandalized on this night, for it is written, 'I will strike *the* pastor, and *the* sheep will be scattered.'[45]

14:28 *sed posteaquam resurrexero praecedam vos in Galilaeam*

"Yet after I rise again, I will go before you to Galilee."

14:29 *Petrus autem ait ei et si omnes scandalizati fuerint sed non ego*

But Peter said to him, "Even if all are scandalized, yet I *will* not *be*!

14:30 *et ait illi Iesus amen dico tibi quia tu hodie in nocte hac priusquam bis gallus vocem dederit ter me es negaturus*

---

[45] See Zechariah 13:7.

And Jesus said to him, "I say to you that you, today – on this night, before *the* rooster gives voice twice – you will deny me three *times*.

14:31 *at ille amplius loquebatur et si oportuerit me simul conmori tibi non te negabo similiter autem et omnes dicebant*

And he spoke further, "Even if it's necessary for me to die with you, I won't deny you."

But they all said *the* same.

In Gethsemani
14:32 *et veniunt in praedium cui nomen Gethsemani et ait discipulis suis sedete hic donec orem*

And they come to *a* farm whose name was Gethsemani. And he said to his disciples, "Sit here while I pray."

14:33 *et adsumit Petrum et Iacobum et Iohannem secum et coepit pavere et taedere*

And he takes Peter, and Jacob, and John with him. And he began to be afraid and tired.

14:34 *et ait illis tristis est anima mea usque ad mortem sustinete hic et vigilate*

And he said to them, "My soul is sad, even to death. Wait here and keep watch."

14:35 *et cum processisset paululum procidit super terram et orabat ut si fieri posset transiret ab eo hora*

And when he had gone apart *a* little, he throws himself on *the* ground and prayed that, if *it* could be, *the* hour could pass away from him.

14:36 *et dixit Abba Pater omnia possibilia tibi sunt transfer calicem hunc a me sed non quod ego volo sed quod tu*

And he said, "Abba, Father, all *these* are possible to you. Take this cup away from me! Yet not what I want, yet what you *want*."

ei

14:37 *et venit et invenit eos dormientes et ait Petro Simon dormis non potuisti una hora vigilare*

And he came and found them sleeping. And he said to Peter, "Simon, are you asleep? Couldn't you keep watch one hour?

And coming back again, he found them sleeping – for their eyes were heavy. And they didn't know what to say to him.

14:38 *vigilate et orate ut non intretis in temptationem spiritus quidem promptus caro vero infirma*

"Keep watch, and pray that you don't enter into testing! *The* spirit indeed is ready, yet *the* flesh is weak."

14:41 *et venit tertio et ait illis dormite iam et requiescite sufficit venit hora ecce traditur Filius hominis in manus peccatorum*

And he came *a* third time, and said to them, "Sleep on, and rest! It's enough. *The* hour has come. Look, man's Son is betrayed into sinners' hands.

14:39 *et iterum abiens oravit eundem sermonem dicens*

And going away he prayed again, saying *the* same word.

14:42 *surgite eamus ecce qui me tradit prope est*

"Get up! Let's go! Look, *the one* who hands me over is near."

14:40 *et reversus denuo invenit eos dormientes erant enim oculi illorum ingravati et ignorabant quid responderent*

Judas Betrays Jesus
14:43 *et adhuc eo loquente venit Iudas Scarioth unus ex duodecim et cum illo turba cum gladiis et lignis a summis sacerdotibus et a scribis et a*

senioribus

And while he *was* speaking, Judas Scarioth came, one of *the* twelve, and with him a crowd with swords and sticks, from *the* high priests and writers and elders.

14:44 *dederat autem traditor eius signum eis dicens quemcumque osculatus fuero ipse est tenete eum et ducite*

But *the* traitor had give his sign to them, saying, "Whomever I kiss, he is *the* one. Arrest him and take *him* away."

14:45 *et cum venisset statim accedens ad eum ait rabbi et osculatus est eum*

And when he had come, coming close to him at once, he said, "Rabbi," and kissed him.

14:46 *at illi manus iniecerunt in eum et tenuerunt eum*

And they laid hands on him and arrested him.

14:47 *unus autem quidam de circumstantibus educens gladium percussit servum summi sacerdotis et amputavit illi auriculam*

But one of those standing around, drawing *a* sword, struck *the* high priest's slave and cut off his ear.

14:48 *et respondens Iesus ait illis tamquam ad latronem existis cum gladiis et lignis conprehendere me*

And Jesus, answering, said to them, "Have you come out to arrest me as if to *a* bandit, with swords and sticks?

14:49 *cotidie eram apud vos in templo docens et non me tenuistis sed ut adimpleantur scripturae*

"I was with you daily in *the* temple, teaching, and you didn't arrest me. Yet so scriptures can be fulfilled . . ."

14:50 *tunc discipuli eius relinquentes eum omnes fugerunt*

Then all his disciples, leaving him, ran away.

A Certain Youth

14:51 *adulescens autem quidam sequebatur illum amictus sindone super nudo et tenuerunt eum*

But *a* certain youth followed him, wearing *a* fine linen cloth over his naked body. And they grabbed him,

14:52 *at ille reiecta sindone nudus profugit ab eis*

and he, throwing off *the* cloth, runs away from them naked.

Jesus On Trial

14:53 *et adduxerunt Iesum ad summum sacerdotem et conveniunt omnes sacerdotes et scribae et seniores*

And they led Jesus to *the* high priest, and all *the* priests and writers and elders come together.

14:54 *Petrus autem a longe secutus est eum usque intro in atrium summi sacerdotis et sedebat cum ministris et calefaciebat se ad ignem*

But Peter followed him far off, even into *the* high priest's courtyard. And he sat with *the* ministers, and warmed himself at *the* fire.

14:55 *summi vero sacerdotes et omne concilium quaerebant adversum Iesum testimonium ut eum morti traderent nec inveniebant*

Indeed, *the* high priests and all *the* council sought testimony against Jesus, so they could give him over to death – yet they weren't finding *it*.

14:56 *multi enim testimonium falsum dicebant adversus eum et convenientia testimonia non erant*

For many spoke false testimony against him, and *the*

testimonies weren't coming together.

14:57 *et quidam surgentes falsum testimonium ferebant adversus eum dicentes*

And certain *individuals* stood up, bringing false testimony against him, saying

14:58 *quoniam nos audivimus eum dicentem ego dissolvam templum hoc manufactum et per triduum aliud non manufactum aedificabo*

that, "We've heard him saying, 'I will dissolve this temple made by hands and, through three days, will build another not made by hands.'"

14:59 *et non erat conveniens testimonium illorum*

And their testimony wasn't coming together.

14:60 *et exsurgens summus sacerdos in medium interrogavit Iesum dicens non respondes quicquam ad ea*

quae tibi obiciuntur ab his

And *the* high priest, standing up in the middle, questioned Jesus, saying, "Aren't you answering anything to these *things* that are thrown up against you by them?"

14:61 *ille autem tacebat et nihil respondit rursum summus sacerdos interrogabat eum et dicit ei tu es Christus Filius Benedicti*

But he kept silent and said nothing. *The* high priest questioned him again, and he says to him, "Are you Christ, *the* Blessed *One's* Son?"

14:62 *Iesus autem dixit illi ego sum et videbitis Filium hominis a dextris sedentem Virtutis et venientem cum nubibus caeli*

But Jesus said to him, "I am, and you will see man's Son sitting at Power's right, and coming with *the* sky's clouds."

14:63 *summus autem*

sacerdos scindens vestimenta sua ait quid adhuc desideramus testes

But *the* high priest, tearing his clothes,[46] said, "Why do we still want witnesses?

14:64 *audistis blasphemiam quid vobis videtur qui omnes condemnaverunt eum esse reum mortis*

"You've heard *the* blasphemy. What does it seem like to you?"

They[47] all condemned him to be guilty of death

14:65 *et coeperunt quidam conspuere eum et velare faciem eius et colaphis eum caedere et dicere ei prophetiza et ministri alapis eum caedebant*

And some began to spit on him, and to cover his face, and hit him with fists, and say to him, "Prophesy!"

And *the* ministers slapped him with *their* hands.

Peter Denies Him
14:66 *et cum esset Petrus in atrio deorsum venit una ex ancillis summi sacerdotis*

And when Peter was in *the* courtyard beneath, one of *the* high priest's female slaves came *down*.

14:67 *et cum vidisset Petrum calefacientem se aspiciens illum ait et tu cum Iesu Nazareno eras*

And when she'd seen Peter warming himself, looking at him, she said, "You were with Jesus Nazarene too."

14:68 *at ille negavit dicens neque scio neque novi quid dicas et exiit foras ante atrium et gallus cantavit*

---

[46] Tearing one's clothing was a sign of grief.

[47] Literally, "Who all condemned . . ."

And he denied it, saying, "I neither know nor understood what you're saying."

And he went outside, in front of *the* courtyard, and *the* cock crowed.

14:69 *rursus autem cum vidisset illum ancilla coepit dicere circumstantibus quia hic ex illis est*

But when *the* slave girl had seen him again, she began to say to those standing around that, "This is one of them."

14:70 *at ille iterum negavit et post pusillum rursus qui adstabant dicebant Petro vere ex illis es nam et Galilaeus es*

And he denied it again. And after *a* little while, those who stood around said to Peter, "You really are *one* of them, for you're Galilean."

14:71 *ille autem coepit anathematizare et iurare quia nescio hominem istum quem dicitis*

But he began to curse and swear that, "I don't know this man whom you're talking *about!*"

14:72 *et statim iterum gallus cantavit et recordatus est Petrus verbi quod dixerat ei Iesus priusquam gallus cantet bis ter me negabis et coepit flere*

And immediately *the* rooster crowed again. And Peter remembered *the* word that Jesus had said to him, "Before *the* rooster crows twice, you'll deny me three *times*" – and he began to weep.

Jesus Before Pilate
Mark 15:1 *et confestim mane
consilium facientes summi
sacerdotes cum senioribus et
scribis et universo concilio
vincientes Iesum duxerunt et
tradiderunt Pilato*

And immediately at morning,
the chief priests, working
counsel with *the* elders and
writers and *the* whole council,
chaining Jesus, led him and
handed him over to Pilate.

15:2 *et interrogavit eum
Pilatus tu es rex Iudaeorum at
ille respondens ait illi tu dicis*

And Pilate asked him, "Are
you *the* Jews' king?"

And he, answering, said to
him, "You say."

15:3 *et accusabant eum
summi sacerdotes in multis*

And *the* chief priests accused
him of many *things*.

15:4 *Pilatus autem rursum
interrogavit eum dicens non*

*respondes quicquam vide in
quantis te accusant*

But Pilate again asked him,
saying, "Aren't you answering
anything? See how many
things they accuse you *of*!"

15:5 *Iesus autem amplius
nihil respondit ita ut miraretur
Pilatus*

But Jesus answered nothing all
the more, so that Pilate is
amazed.

Pilate Releases Barabbas
15:6 *per diem autem festum
dimittere solebat illis unum ex
vinctis quemcumque petissent*

But through *the* feast day, he
was accustomed to set free to
them one of *the* captives,
whomever they had chosen.

15:7 *erat autem qui dicebatur
Barabbas qui cum seditiosis
erat vinctus qui in seditione
fecerant homicidium*

But one was *there* who was
called Barabbas, who was

chained with *the* rebels who had committed murder in *the* rebellion.

15:8 *et cum ascendisset turba coepit rogare sicut semper faciebat illis*

And when *the* crowd had come up, it began to ask what he always did for them.

15:9 *Pilatus autem respondit eis et dixit vultis dimittam vobis regem Iudaeorum*

But Pilate answered them and said, "Do you want that I release *the* Jews' king to you?" –

15:10 *sciebat enim quod per invidiam tradidissent eum summi sacerdotes*

for he knew that *the* high priests had handed him over out of envy.

15:11 *pontifices autem concitaverunt turbam ut magis Barabban dimitteret eis*

But *the* chief priests stirred up *the* crowd more that he release Barabbas to them.

15:12 *Pilatus autem iterum respondens ait illis quid ergo vultis faciam regi Iudaeorum*

But Pilate, again responding, said to them, "What, then, do you want that I do to *the* Jews' king?"

15:13 *at illi iterum clamaverunt crucifige eum*

And again they shouted, "Crucify him!"

15:14 *Pilatus vero dicebat eis quid enim mali fecit at illi magis clamabant crucifige eum*

Indeed Pilate said to them, "Why? For what harm has he done?"

And they shouted more, "Crucify him!"

15:15 *Pilatus autem volens populo satisfacere dimisit illis*

Barabban et tradidit Iesum flagellis caesum ut crucifigeretur

But Pilate, wanting to satisfy *the* people, released Barabbas to them. And he handed Jesus over to beating by *a* whip, so he could be crucified.

Jesus Mocked and Beaten

15:16 *milites autem duxerunt eum intro in atrium praetorii et convocant totam cohortem*

But *the* soldiers led him into *the* headquarters' courtyard, and they call together *the* whole detachment.

15:17 *et induunt eum purpuram et inponunt ei plectentes spineam coronam*

And they dress him in purple and, weaving *a* crown of thorns, they put *it* on him.

15:18 *et coeperunt salutare eum have rex Iudaeorum*

And they began to salute him, "Hail, king of *the* Jews!"

15:19 *et percutiebant caput eius harundine et conspuebant eum et ponentes genua adorabant eum*

And they struck his head with *a* cane, and spat on him, and, falling on *their* knees, they worshiped him.

15:20 *et postquam inluserunt ei exuerunt illum purpuram et induerunt eum vestimentis suis et educunt illum ut crucifigerent eum*

And after they mocked him, they took *the* purple off him and dressed him in his own clothes. And they led him out so they could crucify him.

15:21 *et angariaverunt praetereuntem quempiam Simonem Cyreneum venientem de villa patrem Alexandri et Rufi ut tolleret crucem eius*

And they forced *a* certain passerby, Simon Cyrene, coming from *the* country – Alexander and Rufus's father – that he carry his cross.

The Crucifixion

15:22 *et perducunt illum in Golgotha locum quod est interpretatum Calvariae locus*

And they bring him to *the* place of Golgotha, that is, interpreted, "place of *the* Skull."

15:23 *et dabant ei bibere murratum vinum et non accepit*

And they gave him wine with myrrh[48] to drink, and he didn't take it.

15:24 *et crucifigentes eum diviserunt vestimenta eius mittentes sortem super eis quis quid tolleret*

And crucifying him, they divided his clothes, casting lots over them – who would take what.

15:25 *erat autem hora tertia*

---

[48] Wine with myrrh was offered as an anesthetic, to numb the intense pain of crucifixion.

et crucifixerunt eum

But *it* was *the* third hour, and they crucified him.

15:26 *et erat titulus causae eius inscriptus rex Iudaeorum*

And *the* title of his cause was written, "*The* Jews' king."

15:27 *et cum eo crucifigunt duos latrones unum a dextris et alium a sinistris eius*

And they crucified two bandits with him, one at *the* right, and *the* other at his left.

15:28 *et adimpleta est scriptura quae dicit et cum iniquis reputatus est*

And scripture was fulfilled that says, "And he was considered with *the* treacherous."[49]

Passersby Revile Him on the Cross

15:29 *et praetereuntes*

---

[49] Isaiah 53:12.

*blasphemabant eum moventes
capita sua et dicentes va qui
destruit templum et in tribus
diebus aedificat*

And passersby blasphemed him, shaking their heads and saying, "Ha! Who destroys *the* temple and builds it in three days!

15:30 *salvum fac temet ipsum
descendens de cruce*

"Make yourself safe, coming down from *the* cross!"

15:31 *similiter et summi
sacerdotes ludentes ad
alterutrum cum scribis
dicebant alios salvos fecit se
ipsum non potest salvum
facere*

Likewise also *the* high priests, joking to each other with *the* writers, said, "He made others safe. He can't make himself safe.

15:32 *Christus rex Israhel
descendat nunc de cruce ut
videamus et credamus et qui*

*cum eo crucifixi erant
conviciabantur ei*

"Let Christ, Israel's king, come down now from *the* cross so we can see and believe!"

And *those* who were crucified with him jeered at him.

Jesus Dies in Agony

15:33 *et facta hora sexta
tenebrae factae sunt per totam
terram usque in horam nonam*

And *once the* sixth hour *had* come, shadows came over *the* whole land until *the* ninth hour.

15:34 *et hora nona
exclamavit Iesus voce magna
dicens Heloi Heloi lama
sabacthani quod est
interpretatum Deus meus Deus
meus ut quid dereliquisti me*

And at *the* ninth hour, Jesus shouted in *a* great voice, saying, "Eloi, Eloi, lama sabacthani," that is, interpreted, "My God, My

God, so why have you abandoned me?"[50]

15:35 *et quidam de circumstantibus audientes dicebant ecce Heliam vocat*

And some of those standing around, hearing *him*, said, "Look, he's calling Elijah!"

15:36 *currens autem unus et implens spongiam aceto circumponensque calamo potum dabat ei dicens sinite videamus si veniat Helias ad deponendum eum*

But one, running and filling *a* sponge with vinegar and putting it on *a* stick, gave him *a* drink, saying, "Let *him*! Let's see if Elijah comes to take him down."

15:37 *Iesus autem emissa voce magna exspiravit*

But Jesus, giving out *a* great shout, died.

---

[50] Psalm 22:1.

15:38 *et velum templi scissum est in duo a sursum usque deorsum*

And *the* temple's curtain was torn in two, from above even to below.

15:39 *videns autem centurio qui ex adverso stabat quia sic clamans exspirasset ait vere homo hic Filius Dei erat*

But *the* centurion who stood across, seeing that he had died shouting so, said, "Indeed, this man was God's Son."

The Women Look On
15:40 *erant autem et mulieres de longe aspicientes inter quas et Maria Magdalene et Maria Iacobi minoris et Ioseph mater et Salome*

But *the* woman too were looking on from far off, among whom also *were* Mary Magdalene, and Mary *the* mother of *the* younger Jacob and of Joseph, and Salome.

15:41 *et cum esset in*

Galilaea sequebantur eum et ministrabant ei et aliae multae quae simul cum eo ascenderant Hierosolyma

And when he was in Galilee, they followed him and ministered to him, and many others who came up to Jerusalem together with him.

Jesus Is Buried

15:42 *et cum iam sero esset factum quia erat parasceve quod est ante sabbatum*

And when evening had already come, because it was preparation day – that is, before *the* Sabbath –

15:43 *venit Ioseph ab Arimathia nobilis decurio qui et ipse erat expectans regnum Dei et audacter introiit ad Pilatum et petiit corpus Iesu*

Joseph of Arimathea, *a* nobleman of *the* government, who himself was waiting for God's kingdom, came and boldly went in to Pilate, and asked for Jesus's body.

15:44 *Pilatus autem mirabatur si iam obisset et accersito centurione interrogavit eum si iam mortuus esset*

But Pilate wondered whether he had already died. And, *the* centurion summoned, he asked him whether *Jesus* was already dead.

15:45 *et cum cognovisset a centurione donavit corpus Ioseph*

And when he had found out from *the* centurion, he gave *the* body to Joseph.

15:46 *Ioseph autem mercatus sindonem et deponens eum involvit sindone et posuit eum in monumento quod erat excisum de petra et advolvit lapidem ad ostium monumenti*

But Joseph, buying fine linen cloth and taking him down, wrapped him in *the* cloth and put him in *a* tomb that was cut from *the* rock. And he replaced *the* stone at *the* tomb's opening.

15:47 *Maria autem Magdalene et Maria Ioseph aspiciebant ubi poneretur*

But Mary Magdalene and Mary *of* Joseph saw where he was placed.

Power Over Death

Mark 16:1 *et cum transisset sabbatum Maria Magdalene et Maria Iacobi et Salome emerunt aromata ut venientes unguerent eum*

And when *the* Sabbath had passed, Mary Magdalene, and Mary of Jacob, and Salome bought spices so, coming *early*, they could anoint him.

16:2 *et valde mane una sabbatorum veniunt ad monumentum orto iam sole*

And they come to *the* tomb very early on *the* first *day* of *the* Sabbaths, *the* sun already risen.

16:3 *et dicebant ad invicem quis revolvet nobis lapidem ab ostio monumenti*

And they were saying to each other, "Who will roll back *the* stone for us from *the* tomb's opening?"

16:4 *et respicientes vident revolutum lapidem erat quippe* *magnus valde*

And looking, they see *the* stone rolled back – obviously, it was very large.

16:5   *et introeuntes in monumento viderunt iuvenem sedentem in dextris coopertum stola candida et obstipuerunt*

And going into *the* tomb, they saw *a* youth sitting at *the* right, covered in *a* white robe, and they were astounded.

16:6   *qui dicit illis nolite expavescere Iesum quaeritis Nazarenum crucifixum surrexit non est hic ecce locus ubi posuerunt eum*

He[51] says to them, "Don't be afraid! You're looking for Jesus Nazarene crucified. He has risen. He isn't here. Look! *This is the* place where they put him.

16:7   *sed ite et dicite*

---

[51] Literally, "Who says to them . . ."

discipulis eius et Petro quia praecedit vos in Galilaeam ibi eum videbitis sicut dixit vobis

"Yet go and say to his disciples and to Peter that he's gone before you to Galilee. You will see him there, as he said to you."

16:8   *at illae exeuntes fugerunt de monumento invaserat enim eas tremor et pavor et nemini quicquam dixerunt timebant enim*

And they, going out, ran away from *the* tomb, for trembling and fear had invaded them. And they said nothing to anyone, for they were afraid.

Demonstrations and Disbelief

16:9   *surgens autem mane prima sabbati apparuit primo Mariae Magdalenae de qua eiecerat septem daemonia*

But rising up early *the* first *day* after *the* Sabbath, he appeared first to Mary Madgalene, from whom he'd thrown out seven demons.

16:10 *illa vadens nuntiavit his qui cum eo fuerant lugentibus et flentibus*

She, going *back*, told those who were with him, *while they were* grieving and weeping.

16:11 *et illi audientes quia viveret et visus esset ab ea non crediderunt*

And they, hearing that he was alive and had been seen by her, didn't believe.

16:12 *post haec autem duobus ex eis ambulantibus ostensus est in alia effigie euntibus in villam*

But after this, he showed himself in another form to two of them *while they were* walking, going to *the* country.

16:13 *et illi euntes nuntiaverunt ceteris nec illis crediderunt*

And they, going *back*, told *the* others, yet they didn't believe.

16:14 *novissime recumbentibus illis undecim apparuit et exprobravit incredulitatem illorum et duritiam cordis quia his qui viderant eum resurrexisse non crediderant*

Lastly, he appeared to *the* eleven *while* they *were* reclining *at table*. And he rebuked their disbelief and heart hardness, because they hadn't believed those who had seen him resurrected.

The Risen One Commissions His Disciples

16:15 *et dixit eis euntes in mundum universum praedicate evangelium omni creaturae*

And he said to them, "Going into *the* whole world, preach good news to every creature.

16:16 *qui crediderit et baptizatus fuerit salvus erit qui vero non crediderit condemnabitur*

"Who believes and is baptized will be secured. Indeed, who doesn't believe will be condemned.

16:17 *signa autem eos qui crediderint haec sequentur in nomine meo daemonia eicient linguis loquentur novis*

"But these signs will follow those who believe in my name. They will throw out demons. They will speak new languages.

16:18 *serpentes tollent et si mortiferum quid biberint non eos nocebit super aegrotos manus inponent et bene habebunt*

"They will take up snakes and, if they drink some death-dealing *poison*, it will not harm them. They will lay hands on *the* sick, and they will have health."

The Lord Ascends and the Disciples Set Out

16:19 *et Dominus quidem postquam locutus est eis adsumptus est in caelum et sedit a dextris Dei*

And *the* Lord indeed, after he had spoken to them, was taken up to *the* sky, and sat at God's right.

16:20 *illi autem profecti praedicaverunt ubique Domino cooperante et sermonem confirmante sequentibus signis*

But they, setting out, preached – *the* Lord working with *them* everywhere and confirming *the* words with signs following.

Also in **The Latin Testament Project,**
from Searchlight Press

Searchlight Press
Who are you looking for?
Publishers of thoughtful Christian books since 1994.
info@Searchlight-Press.com
www.Searchlight-Press.com
www.JohnCunyus.com

LaVergne, TN USA
24 June 2010
187237LV00003B/28/P

9 780982 480298